CRAMLINGTON
its past and its people

by Barry Stewart

Text © Barry Stewart, 2014.
First published in the United Kingdom, 2014,
by Stenlake Publishing Ltd.
54–58 Mill Square,
Catrine, Ayrshire, KA5 6RD
Telephone: 01290 551122
www.stenlake.co.uk

ISBN 9781840336542

**The publishers regret that they cannot supply
copies of any pictures featured in this book.**

Acknowledgements

Grateful thanks are due to the following people for advice and the use of material and pictures in this book: Ian Clough, Bob Downer (Blagdon Estates), Kevin Duncan (Durham Mining Museum), Dennis Green, Laura and Ted Hancock, Father Richard Harriott, Julian Harrop (Beamish Museum), Mary Hornsby, Irene Keast, Daphne and Malcolm Morrison, Susan Napier, Betty Norris, Carol Scott (Archivist Northumberland Collections), Jonathan Shaw, Brian Watson – and members of the Cramlington Yesterday and History Societies, past and present, including Albert Foster, Eva James, Alan Lowther, Jack Raffle, Gordon and Alf Smith.

Bibliography

Atkinson, Frank, *The Great Northern Coalfield 1700–1900*, (Newcastle, Frank Graham, 1979).
Davison, John., *Northumberland Miners History 1919–1939* (Cambridge, Buckle, 1973).
Dodds, Madeline Hope, *A History of Northumberland Vol XIII* (Newcastle upon Tyne, Andrew Reid, & Co Ltd., 1930).
Dodd, Peter, (Writing as David Addy), *Dusty Diamonds* (Exeter, Besley and Dalgleish, 1910).
Fynes, Richard, *The Miners of Northumberland and Durham* (Sunderland, Thomas Summerbell, 1873)
Griffin, Andy., *A Slice of Life – Fifty Years in Blyth Valley – The People's Perspective* (Blyth, Blyth Valley Council, 1996)
Hedley, Alan., *Arcot Hall – The First 100 Years* (Newcastle, Image Visual Communications, 2010).
Hutcherson, Margaret, *Let No Wheels Turn – The wrecking of the Flying Scotsman, 1926*, (Washington, TUPS Books, 2006).
Livingstone, A.E. *The Concise Oxford Dictionary of the Christian Church* (Oxford, OUP, 1977).
Lowther, Alan, *Cramlingtuna* (Wooler, Glen Graphics, 1999).
Muckle, William, *No Regrets* (Newcastle, People's Publications, 1981).
Northumberland County Council, *Plessey, The Story of a Northumberland Woodland*, (Hexham, N.C.C., 1984).
Nichol, Basil., *A Guide to the Stained Glass Windows at St. Nicholas Church Cramlington* (Cramlington, St Nicholas Church, 2000).
Simpson, W., *Short History of the Cramlington District Co-operative Society Limited Jubilee Souvenir 1861–1911* (Manchester, CWS, 1912).
Smith, Alf., *Cramlington Through the Ages*, (Wooler, Glen Graphics, 2009).
Tuck, James., *The Collieries of Northumberland Vol 1* (Newcastle, Trade Union Press Services, 1993).
Watson, Geoffrey, *Northumberland Villages* (London, Robert Hale, 1976).
Whellan, W. Histroy, *Topography and Directory of Northumberland* (London, Whellan, 1855).
Brannigan, Patrick, *A Senior Citizen Goes to College* (Unpublished Memoir).
Clough, Ian, *The Effervescent Cloughs of West Cramlington*, (Newcastle, 2010).
Fordyce, *Historical Register of Remarkable Events* (Newcastle, 1872
Gatherer, Michael, *A Guide to the Church of St. John the Baptist – Throughout the Years*, (Cramlington, St. John the Baptist, 1996)
Hancock, Thomas, *Unpublished History of the Hancock Family of Cramlington* (November 1983)
Laverick, J.G. *Souvenir Brochure of the Opening of Cramlington Methodist Church*, (Cramlington, 1969).
Linsley, S.M. *Industrial Archaeological report* (Newcastle, University of Newcastle upon Tyne,1975).
Taylor, H.A. *Cramlington – Historical Survey* (Newcastle, County Hall, 1963).
Colliery Engineering – http:/www dmm.org.colleng/3o23-01 htm
Newcastle Weekly Chronicle: 6th July1873; 2nd August 1873; 9th August 1873.
Sunday Sun 14th February 1958.

INTRODUCTION

The main period covered in this history of Cramlington is the 140 years from the turn of the 19th century. Nationally, this was a time of vast social change and political challenge during the reign of six monarchs, 46 governments and 28 Prime Ministers. For much of the period, Queen Victoria and King Edward VII reigned. Their governments brought in many legislative changes affecting the mines, factories, railways, cereal pricing, suffrage and electoral reform and were responsible for changes in the delivery of education, the organisation of the British Army, the Civil Service and the Trade Unions. During the time covered, the country was led into the Crimean War and two Boer Wars and then the Great World War in Europe. Governments faced the vexed questions of Home Rule for Ireland and the challenges of economic uncertainty following the industrial action of the General Strike (1926) and then the Wall Street crash (1929). Public health was also a major concern during the Spanish flu pandemic of 1918 and 1919 which claimed millions of lives across Europe. Advances were made in air flight. Wireless transmissions were broadcast commercially for the first time. There were new opportunities for working class people to obtain an education and all manner of new learning helped them push at previously inflexible social boundaries.

For a long time, however, particularly at the beginning of Cramlington's history, world and national events would have had little impact on the local social situation. For the most part, ill-educated and poorly informed people in Cramlington, if they knew what was going on at national level, probably considered themselves too remote to be players in the great schemes of government. They had enough to concern themselves with in providing for their families. This book is about those mainly ordinary people who toiled and laboured, mostly in the pits, and brought up their families under hard circumstances and thus in different ways achieved greatness. It is about honouring these people and their past and acknowledging the part they played in creating our present and our future.

In assembling this book, I have been fortunate to have had access to some of the papers collected and collated, over many years, by the Cramlington History and Yesterday Societies. Among these was a handwritten note, drafted by Alan Lowther, a founding member of both groups. Throughout his productive and studious life, he was passionate about learning and local history, particularly about Cramlington. Written in 2002 his note was about the importance of historical and traditional knowledge: *For any community, the store of traditional knowledge, which has been accumulated over the years, should be regarded as a valuable asset. In a sense, it acts as a mirror, reflecting the on-going process of development and change in the social pattern of local life. It is a repository of folk wisdom derived from generations of practical experience of those adapting to living conditions. It provides an insight into the understanding and interpretation of the local scene, containing much that explains communal modes of thought, outlook and action. In fundamental, perhaps unobtrusive ways, such knowledge influences, to a considerable extent, the nurturing of each successive generation. An awareness of this rich source helps contribute to the creation of identity needful for a socially healthy community. This does not imply that we should dwell over much on the past. On the contrary, it implies that awareness and understanding of the past gives community a firmer base and consequently a clearer sense of purpose, ready to face up to and adapt to challenges of contemporary life.*

The book draws on archive material, written autobiography and verbal accounts.

CRAMLINGTON

Cramlington lies nine miles north east of Newcastle upon Tyne and five miles west of the North Sea's coast at Blyth. One hundred and fifty years ago the life of Cramlington revolved around its farms. In the 19th and early 20th centuries, deep mines across the developing town became the main employer. When these became less profitable the face of the town changed again and in 1964 Cramlington was given New Town status. The pit heaps were mostly remodelled and around the existing village large housing estates were built. In the 21st century, only discerning visitors and those who wonder about the abundance of conifers on slightly elevated ground will recognise the town's industrial heritage.

Cramlington has an interesting history. Its name is thought to be derived from '*Kramel*' the conquering Viking who held land in the area as agent for the ruler. The connecting word '*ing*' in the name of the town, which signifies protectorate of men of the same kin, was added and later the ending '*ton*', which means enclosure. Through time, '*Kramelington*'[1] became Cramlington.

In feudal times, the Barony of Cramlington and the hamlet of Whitlawe formed part of the Barony of Ellingham, which was owned by Nicholas de Grenville. Cramlington later passed to the Gaugy family who were Lords of Jesmond. The Book of Fees for 1135 shows that Cramlington was held by a family bearing the name William de Cramlington.

The first chapel in the Manor can be traced to the period between 1163 and 1180 when it was under the stewardship of 'John de Clerk' of Cramlington.[2]

For over 600 years without interruption thereafter, Cramlington enjoyed agricultural stability. Records show that in 1242 the meadow and arable land of Cramlington were considered to be good and could be let annually for a rent of 105 gallons of wine.

In 1270, Adam of Jesmond, who was then the owner of Cramlington, was granted permission from the king to hold a weekly market. This suggests rising land value and a thriving community which by the end of that century had notable residents, including Adam the reeve, William the chaplain, Thomas the brewer, Roger the miller and seven other tenant farmers.

By 1298 arable land was worth sixpence an acre annually and the cost of renting the windmill, situated to the north west of the village, was 3s 4d. a year. By 1420 Cramlington was back under the ownership of William Cramlington.

By 1466 the Manorial rights of the village were divided and were held by William's two daughters, Alice and Agnes, who had married into separate branches of the Lawson family. Together these families took responsibility for repairing the chapel, which was then described as being '*barn-like with round leaded windows with shutters and thick stone walls.*'

In 1665 the system of Parish Register began, and in 1680 the church of St. Nicholas was rebuilt on the site of an earlier Norman chapel.

John Brand, perpetual curate of Cramlington and historian of Newcastle, records that in 1778, 'Presentation' to St. Nicholas Church was made by Sir Matthew White Ridley of Blagdon Hall, who was M.P. for Newcastle upon Tyne; and John Lawson Esquire. For centuries, 'Rights of Presentation and Advowson' could be bought and sold like any other property. Sir Matthew's share in the parish had been purchased earlier that century.

---

[1] Watson, Godfrey, *Northumberland Villages* (London, Robert Hale, 1796) p.111 suggests that Cramlington derives its name from Crane's Spring, but in this contention, he appears to be almost in a singular minority.

[2] It is pleasing to note that in 2013, in recognition of this, the former Travellers' Rest public house in the village (built by Thomas Doughty in 1903) was given the name 'John the Clerk of Cramlington'.

Cramlington Hall was built in the mid 18th century by John Lawson of West Cramlington on a site which had been occupied by previous hall buildings. Lawson died without children and under the terms of his will, through a succession of complex arrangements involving the priest Thomas Lawson and Robert Storey, the estate passed to a distant cousin, Adam Mansfeldt de Cardonnel. In accordance with the bequest made to him, Cardonnel changed his name to Lawson.[3] The hall was sold to Sir Matthew White Ridley in 1834 and in 1934 to Mr. and Mrs. Brooks.[4]

George Shum served or adventured in India and is believed to have been an army medical man and is said to have been physician to the Nabob of Arcot – Arcot being a fortified town near Madras. Arcot was seized by Clive of India in 1751, who then beat off a series of French attacks and although it was eventually retaken by the French, it was recovered in 1760 and it's widely reported as laying the basis of British supremacy in India. Details of Shum's involvement in these events are unclear but what is certain is that he returned to the North East, possibly about 1796 … reputedly in possession of a bag of emeralds, believed to be a gift from a grateful Nabob whose life Shum is said to have saved. Possibly the booty was simply the spoils of war … Shum bought land from Robert Storey … courted and (in 1822), married Storey's daughter Ann. In deference to her father's wishes, he assumed the name Shum-Storey. [5]

The illustration[6] above shows one of the original pillars from the Norman chapel.

---

[3] For a detailed account of the early history of Cramlington and the transfer of rights and land see Dodds, Madeline Hope, *A History of Northumberland* Vol. XIII (Newcastle upon Tyne, Andrew Reid & Co Ltd. 1930) pp. 386–389.
[4] Smith, Alf, *Cramlington Through the Ages*, (Wooler, Glen Graphics, 2009) pp. 11–13.
[5] Hedley, Alan, *Arcot Hall – The First 100 Years 1909–2009*, (Newcastle, Image Visual Communications, 2010) pp. 75–76.
[6] Except where otherwise indicated, the photographic images are from the archives of Cramlington Yesterday and History Society, having been lodged with these societies by Mr. Alan Lowther and Mr. Jack Raffle – both now deceased.

In 1803, George Shum-Storey built Arcot House. An un-attributed Northumberland County Council report dated 31st October 1983 described Arcot Hall (as it then was) as a – *Country house ... with a south block which form an L plan with service wings to the north ... three storeys, three symmetrical bays ... central Roman Doric porch with pilasters and triglyph frieze ... lounge (which) retains anthemion cornice ... fireplace flanked by fluted shafts with leafy capitals, carrying lintel with medallions.*

A second report also in possession of Cramlington Yesterday Society adds: *Arcot Hall was built to be a comfortable family home ... with elegant rooms ... with a small chapel with an arched window above the lounge.*[7]

Despite the elegance of the house the area surrounding Arcot House (or Hall as it became) was subjected to different forms of mining over many years – bell-pit, drift and board and pillar excavation accessed via various shafts. Occupation of the house, within the family, also changed.

On 12th June 1872, Emmeline Anne Shum Storey, the eldest daughter of Henry Shum Storey, married Captain Shawe of the Royal Marines. This union gave further alteration to the family name – from Shum Storey to Shawe-Storey. The Historical Register of Remarkable Events records that – *Flags of various colours and designs waved from every prominent point within eyeshot of Arcot or Cramlington; guns were fired from the early morning till late evening, and the cheerful music of the Seaton Burn Saxhorn Band augmented the festive character of the proceedings. The bridal party left the hall in seven carriages, each driven by a handsome pair of grey horses, driven by properly costumed equerries. The bride was dressed in white corded satin trimmed with Brussels lace, tulle, and bouquets of orange blossom with tulle and wreath and pearl ornaments. The bridesmaids ... were dressed in white tarlatan trimmed with cerise, Dolly Varden caps and tulle ends and bouquets.* [8]

---

[7] Ref L2g – Arcot Hall.

[8] Fordyce, (Newcastle, 1876) *Historical Register of Remarkable Events – The marriage of Emmeline Anne Shum-Storey to Captain Shawe – 12th June 1872.*

THE GROWTH OF CRAMLINGTON AS A VILLAGE

Before the beginning of commercial mining, the early parish of Cramlington comprised 3,492 acres, the boundaries then being Horton Burn in the north, Sandy's Letch, near Dudley in the south, Plessey and Stannington in the west and Seaton Delaval in the east. The highest point of the area, at 273 feet above sea level, is Beacon Hill in the west. In 1801, apart from a small number of agricultural labourers, the village had three shoemakers, two grocers, one tailor, one blacksmith, one cartwright, one carrier and nine farmers. Prior to Cramlington developing as a mining community, the population was 271. By 1821 there were 330 people living in the village in 68 houses, most of which were thatched. One hundred years later there were 8,517 inhabitants.[9] The roads were yet to be laid with tarmac, and footpaths, where they existed, were adopted by common usage on roadside verges or across fields. The image of Station Road shown below was typical.

Arcot House prior to it becoming the club house for the Arcot golf course.

---
[9] The population in 2013 was in excess of 39,000.

Cramlington village in 1890, showing The Fox and Hounds Inn near the church.

A clearer image of The Fox and Hounds Inn.[10]

---

[10] Image from Malcolm and Daphne Morrison's collection.

Opposite Cramlington Hall there was a market garden with walled enclosure. When it closed it was under the stewardship of Mr. Martin Thompson.[11]

Land in Cramlington was under the ownership of four wealthy employers and a map made for the Newcastle Coal District in 1847 shows how the area was divided. In the Plessey region west of Hartford the land was owned by Sir Matthew White Ridley, 4th Baronet.

Sir Matthew White Ridley, Bart.

The area east of Sir Matthew Ridley's land, up the natural boundary created by the River Blyth was owned by Ralph Bates Esquire. On the south side of the river, Sir Matthew owned a further portion of land up to Beacon Hill at Bassington. From there into the central area of Cramlington Thomas Taylor of Cramlington Manor had ownership, but in the East Cramlington sector George Shum Storey retained the rights. Shum Storey also owned the land around Dam Dykes and Arcot Hall where he had his residence. In the south east, towards Seghill and Seaton Delaval, ownership was in the hands of Sir Francis Blake.

---

[11] The gardens were substantial and led west towards the present Sunnyside Estate and south towards Village Surgery. Mr. Thompson's house was close to the present Lal Qila restaurant.
[12] Sir Matthew White Ridley, 4th Baronet of Blagdon (1807–1877). Reproduced with permission of Blagdon Estate.

THE FARMS

In the 18th century there were twelve farms. In the very centre of the village, near the church, were East, Middle and West Farms. Half a mile or so to the west were White Hall and Beacon; slightly to the south were Dam Dykes, Moor and South Farms.

North of the village centre was Crow Hall Farm. There was another West Farm on the western boundary, and towards the River Blyth, East Hartford, Bank Top and West Hartford Farms. Stickley Farm, in the east, was on its own between Seaton Delaval and Horton. East of what became Klondyke, was East Cramlington Farm.

The acreage of these farms in the early 1900s was quite small. For example, East Farm in the centre, with thirteen fields and an orchard, under the tenancy of James Hoy had 216 acres; West Farm nearby and managed by Mr. Iyzack extended west towards Cramlington Railway Station and with fourteen fields, had 209 acres. Crowhall Farm, tenanted by Mr. Turnbull had 20 fields, comprising 120 acres. Some fields at his tenancy were very small and close to the farm house. Subsequently, the boundaries changed and in 1855 the farmers in the town were:

Thomas Bell	Cramlington
John Boutflower	Bassington
Edward Hood	Cramlington Moorhouse
John Lowes	Cramlington Beacon
Ralph Milburn	Dam Dykes
George Riddle	Cramlington Whitehall
Thomas Sisterton	South Cramlington
John Smith	Shankhouse
Thomas Wardle	Cramlington [13]

Two of the farms were owned by Sir Matthew White Ridley; one was owned by George Shum Storey. The others were closely linked to the collieries.

[14]

East Farm and Quarrie House.

---

[13] Smith, *Ibid*, pp. 16–18.
[14] Quarrie House, was named after Andrew Quarrie and his family, and was later owned by Miss Hornsby who gave generously to St. Nicholas Church, other organisations and to people in need.

During the Industrial Revolution there was a huge market for food as urban areas expanded. The spread of railways helped in the transport of produce and farming prospered. Production was very labour intensive. Seeds were sown by hand, farms were small and enclosed and land utilisation involved set-aside sections which were allowed to lie fallow during periods of recovery. During winter it was common to slaughter livestock because there were insufficient stored crops to feed them. Later, following the Dutch example, turnips were planted and these helped restore the land and feed livestock outside the growing season. Stock-breeding also improved, which brought about increased yield of both meat and milk.

Subsequently, the enclosure movement did away with partitioned land making it easier to cultivate on a larger scale. Localised use of wind, water and horse power gave way to steam-driven machinery which, together with knowledge of weed control and fertilisation, increased productivity. However, good times for British farmers began to end when steam-powered sailing vessels began to import cheap grain from America. The First World War added to the problem as the military commandeered nearly all farm horses for war work. In response, the government brought in 5,000 of Henry Ford's tractors. These further added to the demise of traditional methods of agriculture. Prior to all of this, especially in remote areas like Cramlington, farming methods remained labour intensive, and dependent on seasonal and casual workers.

Potato pickers at Shankhouse, *c*.1915.

Bassington Farm.

1 & 2: Middle Farm and its building prior to their conversion to The Plough Public House.
3: West Hartford Farm.
4: Dam Dykes Farm House, built late 17th century.
5: Making hay.
6: Stickley Farm in 1916. Second left is Benjamin Hogg, the tenant.

Ancient stables[15] behind the Blagdon.

S.M. Linsley, staff tutor in Industrial Archaeology at the University of Newcastle upon Tyne, reporting in 1975 on West Farm, Cramlington (formerly known as Elbow Well), described the layout of West Farm: *West Farm comprises two interesting groups of buildings; a linear farmstead incorporating an original farm house to the west, a later farmhouse in the centre and to the east, a pantiled granary with cart shed below. This arrangement is very characteristic of Northumbrian linear farmstead development which typified many of the region's farms from about 1700 onwards. The second grouping, to the north of the first, is of the E shaped plan, which is typical of improved farms being built or reconstructed throughout the region between 1780 and 1850. The circular-plan Gin Gan may be an addition and if so this would suggest that this grouping may be late 18th century or very early 19th century. As a whole, the steading is a splendid example of farmsteads developed in the region between 1700 and 1850.* [16]

Many of the other farms in the town were built on similar lines, but as the 1860s map on page 16 shows, the pattern was not followed exactly.

The lay-out of Plessey Checks (shown on page 19) also provides an alternative configuration.

In a presentation given to Cramlington Yesterday Society on 2nd May 2000, Mr. Alan Lowther provided his account of the farms of Cramlington: *Hall Farm was next to what is now the Lal Qila Indian restaurant. East Farm was known for years as Wardle's Farm. The 1769 map of the village shows farmsteads at Shankhouse, East Cramlington (known locally as High Pit Farm; South Farm, known locally as Botany Bay, and Crow Hall Farm situated where there is now an industrial estate. The last named was the location in the 19th century of a boarding academy run by Reverend W.D. Thompson, curate of Horton.*

Outside the parish boundary lay East Hartford Farm and Stickley Farm (still functioning). A Richard of Stickley is mentioned in the 13th century manorial records as being co-heir of Cramlington.

---

[15] Image (believed to be one of Cramlington's oldest buildings) fom Susan Napier's collection.

[16] S.M. Linsley's report argued in favour of the West Farm building being given 'listed or scheduled' status – which, with proper care, would enhance Cramlington New Town. The buildings presently (2013) provide accomodation for a veterinary surgeon's consulting room; office and surgery rooms and upstairs a chiropractor's suite.

At West Cramlington was the Tilery Farm (where Alexandra Park roundabout is now placed). Dam Dykes and Plantation Farms lie beyond the railway crossing on the road to Arcot Hall. Further north-westwards were Beacon Farm (now a nursing home) and Bassington Farm, sited on the industrial estate of that name.

Whitehall Farm, south west of Beacon Farm, is still a working farm, but urban development is scheduled there. Along the road from the roundabout below Dam Dykes, Barns Farm was located 200 yards west of Moor Farm. Barns Farm gave its name to the Barns Park housing estate. Bassington Bridge Farm was sited north of the railway bridge across the A1068 road on the east side.

The gin-gan, barns and house at West Farm.

The Old Smithy.[17]

In any village a skilled blacksmith or farrier was needed and in Cramlington the smithy was in the centre of the village a few yards to the west of the graveyard of St. Nicholas Church.

---

[17] The Old Smithy was demolished in 1974 but the car park in the village, opposite the main shopping complex, still carries its name.

THE VILLAGE

Prior to 1801, when the village was still a small agricultural settlement, the precise population of Cramlington is not known. However, by 1851 coal mining had changed the area and in that year 694 men and boys, some as young as eight, were employed in Cramlington's coal mines.

Village Square.

DEMOGRAPHIC CHANGES

Over twelve decades, local census data shows how changes in industry, from predominantly farming to mining, brought about a steady increase in the number of residents – as follows:

Year	1811	1821	1831	1841	1851	1861	1871	1881	1891	1901	1911	1921
Population	*280*	*330*	*931*	*2,634*	*3,367*	*3,301*	*4,167*	*5,744*	*5,967*	*6,437*	*8,093*	*8,517*

By 1851, within Cramlington there were over 500 dwellings. The conurbation then embraced: Shankhouse, High Pit, Stone Row, Terrace, Black Garth, East Cramlington, West Cramlington, and Bassington.

Most of the mine workers were natives of Cramlington, but some had migrated from the north of the county from places such as Ancroft and Shilbottle, and from the south of the region, including the areas of Leadgate and Marley Hill.

Under the 1894 Local Government Act, Cramlington was governed by an Urban Development Council. The urban area included East and West Cramlington and Shankhouse. In 1912, East and West Hartford were added and these additional conurbations, along with the growth in mining, account for the increases in population.

The 1860 Ordnance Survey map of Cramlington Village (see overleaf) provides a distinct impression of what the old village looked like. Most of the dwellings ran east to west from St. Nicholas Church. There were three old quarries not far from the two inns – the Blue Bell and the Fox and Hounds. Later the Blue Bell Inn (which by 1889 was the Blagdon Hotel) became the Blagdon Arms. The map shows that outside the main line of houses there was a handful of terraced houses grouped around tree-lined areas. The connecting roadways were narrow and roughly linked. There was a small pond behind the former Wesleyan Chapel and a larger one where the shopping complex car parks are now situated at the north east end of the town.

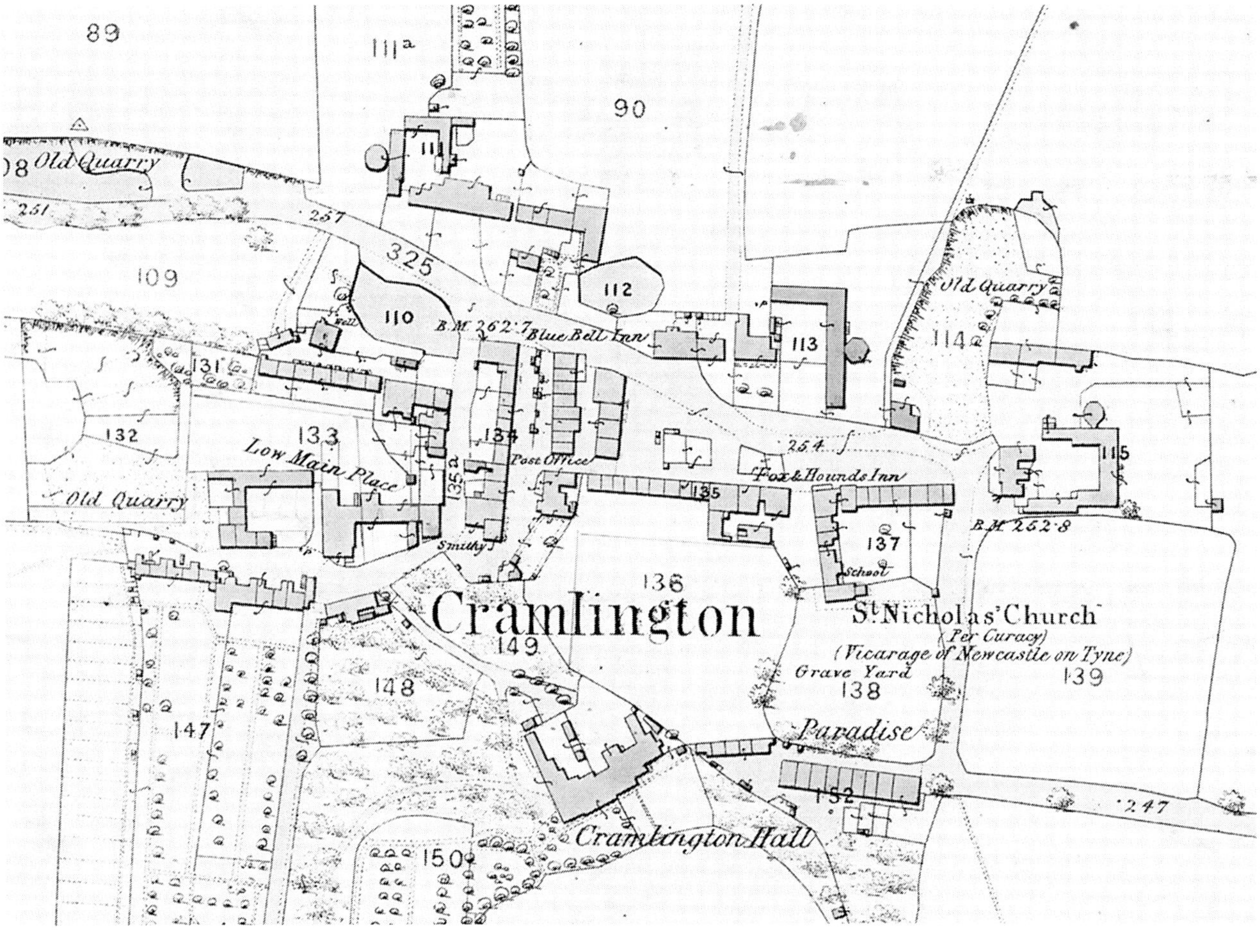

At the bottom of the map, and shown in the early photograph at the foot of the page, is Paradise Row.

These houses have always been in a cul-de-sac because at the west end of the lane is a stone wall. This was alternatively known by local people as either the Feuding Wall or Spite Wall. The name 'Feuding Wall' originated from the belief that the wall was built because of hostility between the richer people living in The Hall and the poorer folk who resided in Paradise Row. The name 'Spite Wall' is thought to have originated from the idea that the 'lower class' tenants of Paradise Row should be made to walk around the village to access points a stone's-throw away, rather than pass directly in front of The Hall. A reporter touring colliery villages in 1873 for *Newcastle Weekly Chronicle*, facetiously described the properties in Paradise Row as 'mansions', saying that they could – *'only have been so named because of their nearness to the church and vicar's house … they are very small … with one room at ground level and an untenable garret up a ladder. To these delectable abodes no conveniences whatever are attached, and there is only one ash pit for the use of all Paradise – and it frequently overflows with the united contributions of the inhabitants. Miserable little hovels are these, and they must either have been built when people had different ideas of what constituted bliss, or the name has been conferred in the bitterness of mockery.'* [19]

---

[18] OS 1st Ed. 080-08 Map reproduced with permission of Northumberland Archives.
[19] Extract from *Newcastle Weekly Chronicle* for Saturday 2nd August, 1873, p.2.

Alan Lowther succinctly captured every-day life from this period (and slightly later), in his poem entitled 'Paradise'.[20]

> 'Between the vicarage grounds and churchyard wall
> Roofs overburdened with their chimney stacks,
> (Great pot-less slabs that belch out curly clouds,
> From fiery hearths heaped up with nutty-slack),
> The roughly mortared walls of Paradise
> Crouch timidly behind water- butts,
> Steps bordered round with yellow-donkey-stone
> In contrast to the pock-marked, muddy street.
> Diminutive-paned windows let in light
> On press, harmonium, top-table plush cloth.
> Round oven doors conceal vast white-washed caves
> Redolent with crisply baking bread.
> Wire cooling racks sag underneath their load
> Of fadges, seedy teacakes, plaited loaves,
> Whilst square sly-cake and crushed apple tarts
> Await their turn to cook for Sunday tea.
> Pit stockings freshly darned in neat criss-cross
> Hang regimented on long brass rail
> That runs beneath the crowded mantelshelf,
> Where candlesticks, tea caddies, china dogs,
> Reflect the flickering light of leaping flames,
> Proudly displaying housewife's treasured taste.
> Barrelled herrings glittering in their salt
> Vie with brown ware, covered water-jar
> And stone of flour in its metal bin
> To fill the dark recess behind the door.
> Underneath the skylight's aperture
> The bedstead with its highly ornate ends
> Carries bolster, pillows, quilted quilt
> All overspread with patterned counterpane.
> Thin legs support a wash stand's marble top,
> With basin, ewer, soap-dish, shaving mug
> Tucked snugly underneath the sloping joists,
> That bear the overlapping, grey-blue slates.
> In furthest corner lurks a cabin trunk,
> Packed full of blankets, rugs and winding sheets,
> The last-named mindful of life's later end,
> Each layer strewn with bits of old clay pipe.
> The shrinking feet are shielded from the chill
> Of arctic oilcloth on the wooden floor
> By bedside multi-coloured clippie mat,
> The work of toiling fingers by lamplight.
> Below the vicarage orchard's high stone
> Trim gardens filled with rows of peas and beans,
> Potatoes, cabbage, scallions, onions, leeks,
> Ensure the dinner pans are well supplied.
> A breezy, sun-clear Monday morning's work,
> Sees lines of washing stretched across the street.
> Black-leading grates and polishing door knobs,
> Shaking mats and scrubbing hearth and floor
> On Fridays make the house spick and span
> For quiet rest from task on Sabbath day.'

---

[20] Lowther, Alan, *Cramlingatuna*, (Wooler, Glen Graphics, 1999) pp.15–16.

The writer of the *Newcastle Weekly Chronicle*, quoted above, had painted a different picture and stated Paradise Row was not alone in its deprivation; indeed in his estimation, Pond Row was worse. He described the slightly better houses in West Cramlington as *'having one room downstairs and one up; the upper being reached by a flight of stone steps outside, and a strange looking gallery in the front.'* [21]

In the same article reference is made to the Post Office, which was the most westerly house in Church Street. The postmaster by this time was Mr. Bowman, who was also telegraph clerk, banker, postman and church clerk. He was not however, the first postman in Cramlington. The first record appears in Whellan's directory of 1855 [22] names the holder of this position as Thomas Bell, who was also a grocer, flour dealer and tenant farmer of Hall Farm belonging to Cramlington Hall.

This farm, of 214 acres and employing six labourers, had been bought from Sir Matthew White Ridley at the turn of the century by Thomas Taylor, Esq. of Chipchase Castle.

'Cramlington … must have been a pleasant place to live (in the 1860s); the Manor hall with trees and gardens, the hall lodge cottage and Hall Close field, a cluster of homes fronting the quarry. … A number of wells producing ice cold water supplied the wants of people and animals.' [23]

The well in the garden of Cramlington Hall.

---

[21] *Newcastle Illustrated Chronicle, Ibid* p.2.
[22] Whellan, W., *History, Topography and Directory of Northumberland*, (London, Whellan, 1855).
[23] Smith, Alf, *Ibid,* p.28.

COAL MINING

The activities of coal mining drained water from the wells and significantly changed the identity of Cramlington. Coal had been mined at Plessey, just north of Cramlington, from the middle of the 13th century, and in the Plessey area, of the 35 pits which had been in operation in 1765, there were thirteen mines, still winning coal, when they closed there in 1813.

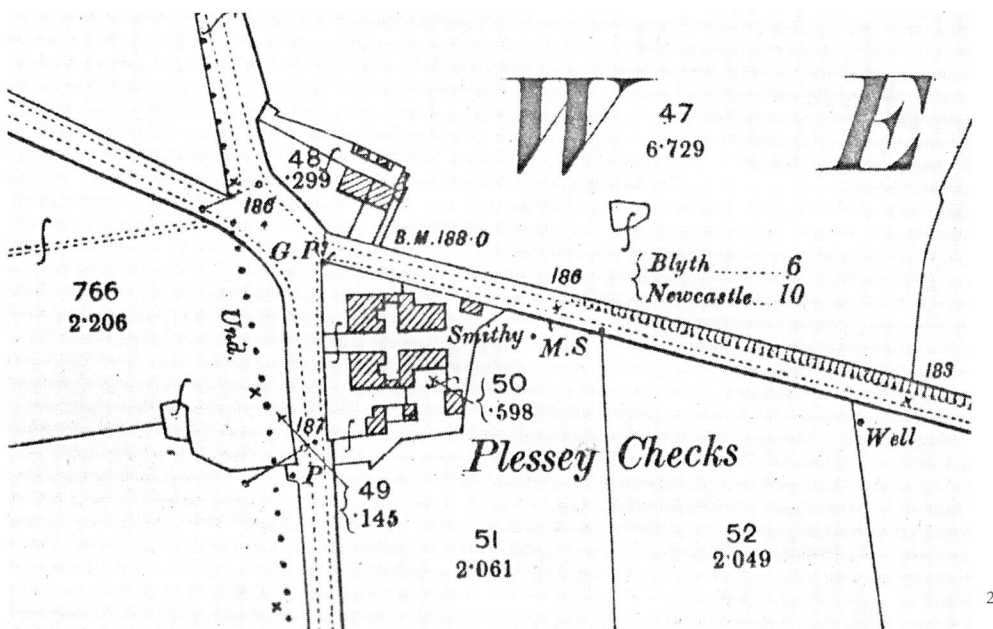

The mining and small farming village at Plessey Checks,[25] with its Three Shires Inn, where the roundabout on the A192 road above Hartford Bridge is now situated, is gone without trace and the wagon-way which led from the collieries is no longer visible.

Farm buildings at Plessey Checks, *c*.1900.

At Plessey there is an east-west geological fault in the earth's structure. This has the effect of throwing the coal seams to the north of the fault some 30-60 feet downwards. The seams of coal on the south side were more easily accessible, and it was on this side that the early pits were first dug. These were 'bell pits' which were dug down until the roof was likely to collapse, whereupon a similar pit on an adjacent or near site was sunk.

---

[24] O.S. 2nd edition 25" map, reproduced with permission of Northumberland Archives.

[25] The name Plessey is derived from the French 'La Place' – Plassay, a reminder that it was the home of a Norman invader. 'Checks' signifies that it was the place where coal wagons surrendered their 'check' to prove they had paid the tariff to use the then privately owned roadway. It was also the place where John Wesley, founder of Methodism, preached when he made his legendary tour of Britain on horseback.

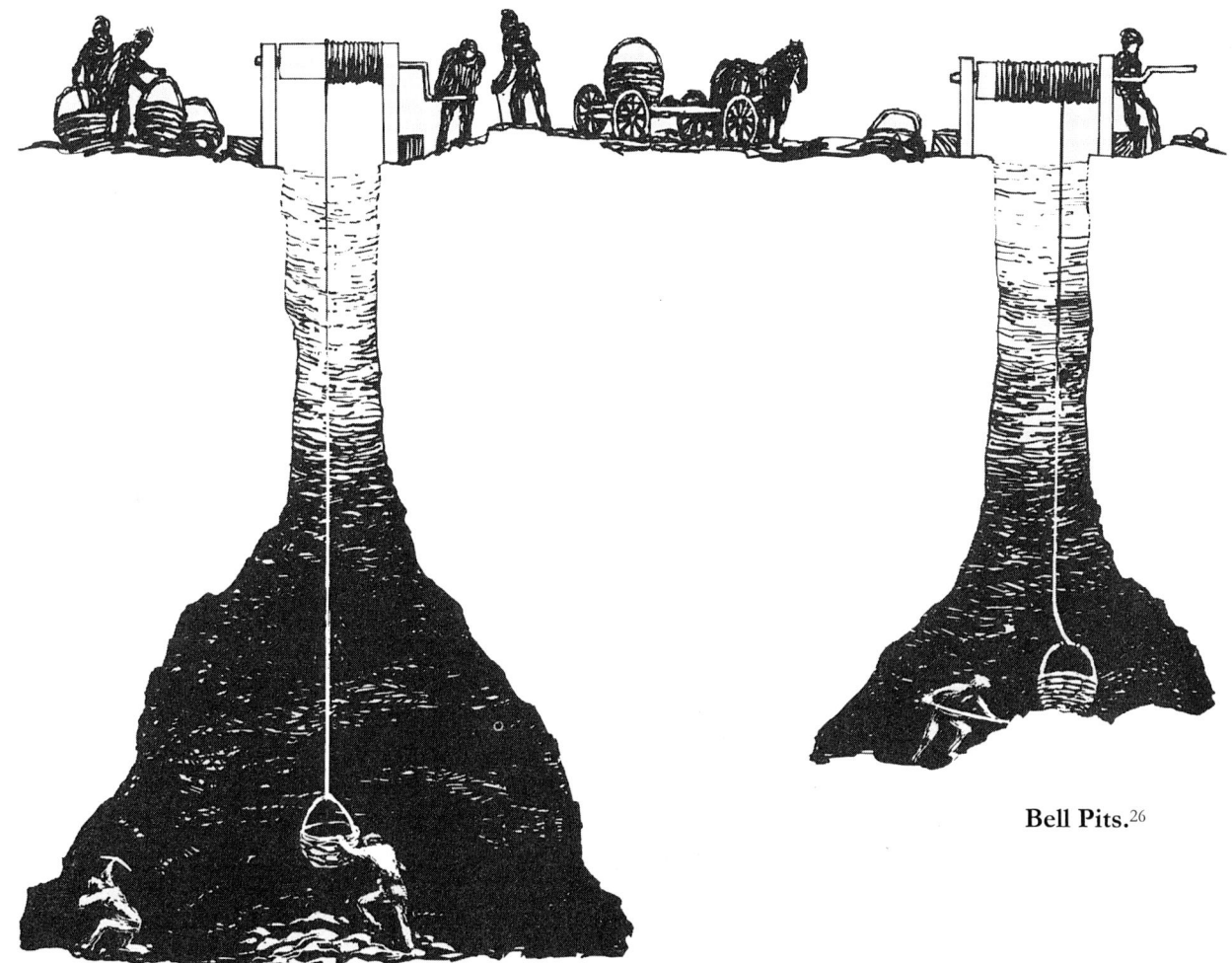

Bell Pits.[26]

Ventilation, in a 'blackdamp' atmosphere, almost without oxygen but with a mixture of carbon monoxide, nitrogen and water vapour, was a major safety issue for the underground workmen.[27] In subsequent pits ventilation shafts and the use of hot air pumped into the depth of the mine, helped circulate oxygen into the underground atmosphere. Drainage was another issue and where mines were connected, if one flooded the others did too. Pumping was necessary. At first this was achieved by the use of horses circulating in a gin gan, turning a wheel onto which a rope and buckets to draw off water were attached. By the early 18th century, pumps were operated by steam or 'fire' engines.[28]

In 1722, to the north and east of the geological fault, collieries were established at West Hartford by Messrs Wright and Spearman of Sedgefield and Hetton.[29] By 1728 Richard Ridley and Company had absorbed the collieries. By 1812, the colliery at West Hartford had closed.

The first mining lease in Cramlington Manor was dated 13th May 1825: this was the beginning of the Cramlington Coal Company. The directors were Joseph Lamb, Edward Potter, William Scott, John Straker and Thomas Barnes. These gentlemen were all well-known businessmen and devout Christians. Originally Mr. Straker was the colliery 'viewer' or manager at East Cramlington and was succeeded by Mr. Potter who lived at Cramlington House on the Klondyke to East Cramlington road.

---

[26] Northumberland County Council, *Plessey, The Story of a Northumberland Woodland* (N.C.C., Hexham, 1984) p.12.

[27] See also Muckle, William, *No Regrets*, (Newcastle, Peopple's Publications, 1981), p.19. *'Many time in my younger day, I would come home and could not eat anything. I would lie on the floor and sleep, dog tired from the bad air down the pit.'*

[28] Muckle, *Ibid*, pp.11–17.

[29] There were three 18th century pits: Well, Rodney and another pit simply named Bassington, close to where all three were located. The *Plessey* booklet specified above provides an outline map on page 14 of where the pits were located in 1765; including the Rodny pit.

Cramlington House had been built by Adam (Mansfeldt de Cardonnel) Lawson in the early 19th century, before becoming the family home of the Potter family. In the early years of the 20th century the occupant was Mr. J. Morrison, and later Mr. T.O. Woods, both of whom were chief engineers of the Cramlington Coal Company. Later Cramlington House became the Coal Board's head office. Cramlington House was demolished in 1969 and Lanercost Park housing estate now occupies the site. The lodge house remains. The lane running north from the Seaton Delaval road is still known locally as 'Potter's Lane.'

Hartley Main Colliery's staff at Cramlington House, with Mr. T.O. Wood (Director) with his overcoat on, and his dog in the front row. Harry Simpson is fifth from the left in the back row.

---

[30] Image provided by Mrs. Irene Keast (daughter of Mr. Harry Simpson).

Following the signing of the mining lease in 1825, Joseph Lamb and his partner Edward Potter sunk shafts at East Cramlington at the Engine Pit, which was located 150 feet above sea level. The shaft went to a depth of 541 feet and encountered coal at seven levels but principally 'won' coal from the High Main, Yard and Hartley seams at depths of 245, 358, 486 feet respectively. During the same period, Joseph Lamb and Edward Potter also sunk the Ann Pit at High Cramlington. In 1837 the Backworth Coal Company sank the pit at West Cramlington, under the ownership of Humble Lamb. In 1847 the Amelia Pit shaft was sunk at Shankhouse, and the Lamb Pit in East Cramlington in 1849. The Richard (or Dicky) Pit (East Cramlington Colliery) was also sunk in 1849. The shaft of the Betsy Pit, close to the Ann Pit, was sunk in 1854. East Hartford collieries, the Athey and Scott were just beyond the parish boundary. Their shafts were sunk in 1858 and 1866 respectively.

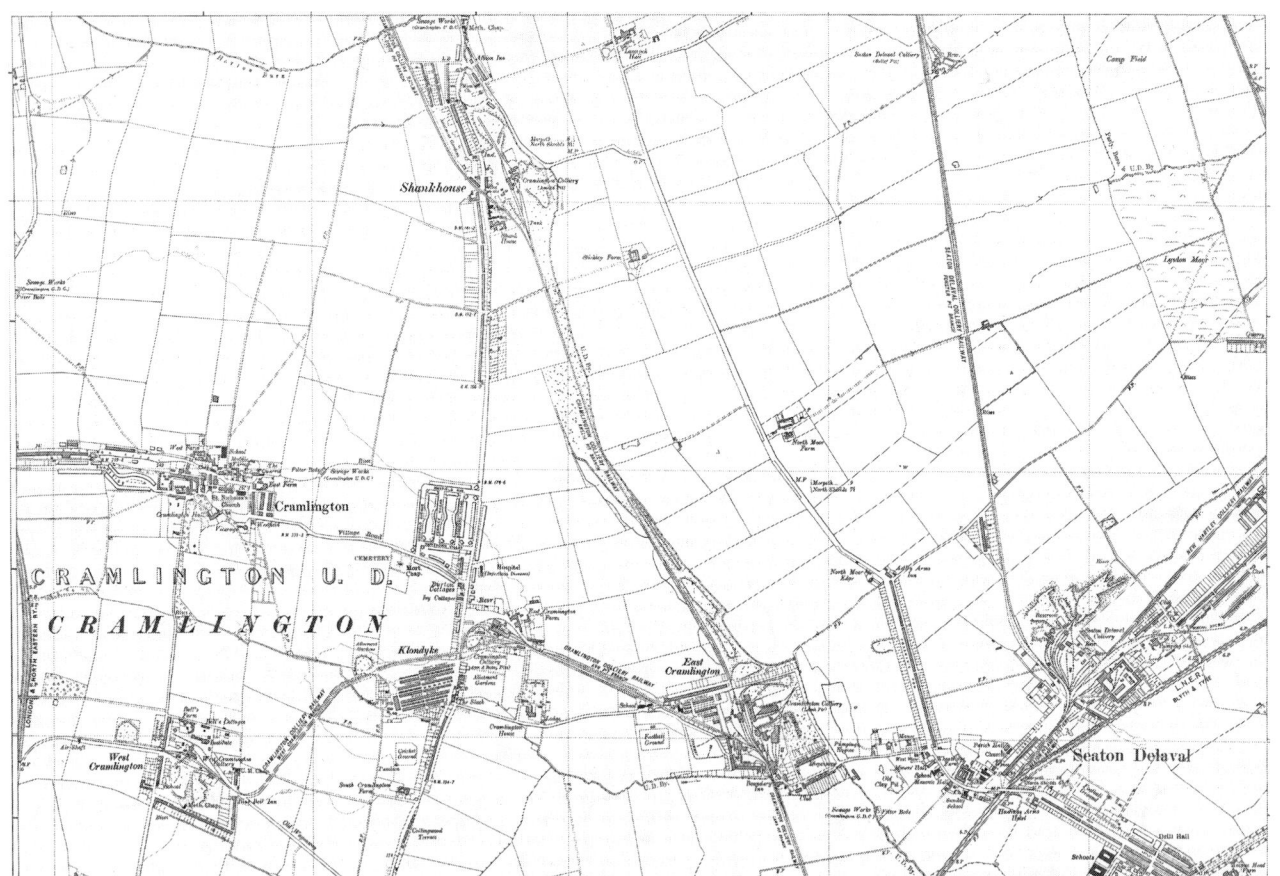[31]

The copy Ordnance Survey map above provides a broad perspective of Cramlington as it was developed as a mining area.

Long or *short* methods of extracting coal were in use in mining from the early 19th century. The former system entailed taking all or most of the accessible coal out of the mine, but only where the strata above and below the coal seam was stable. The more common method was board (or bord) and pillar which entailed leaving a pillar of coal of up to nine yards square in the seam to support the roof. Once the coal was extracted in the initial locality the hewers moved on to an adjoining area of the seam to win coal which was then similarly supported by a pillar. Later the long-wall system of coal extraction was used which entailed leaving long, continuous pillars of the coal seam as the coal face was worked forwards. Evidence of this type of underground working can be clearly seen where pits have been abandoned and the worked, underground areas have collapsed to cause undulating patterns on the surface across farm fields.

---

[31] O.S. Map 1938 edition reproduced with permission of Northumberland Archives.

THE COLLIERIES

The 'Ann'[32] ('Annie' or 'Anne' Pit as it is sometimes incorrectly named on some maps and mining correspondence) was situated approximately 100 yards west of East Cramlington Farm House in the village, near High Pit. It was sunk on 28th February 1825[33] to a depth of 482 feet and was alternatively known as High Pit. Borings revealed several layers of coal, two of which were workable. These were the High seam which was 4 feet 11 inches high and 115 feet from the surface; and the Main seam of 5 feet 7 inches at the very bottom of the shaft.

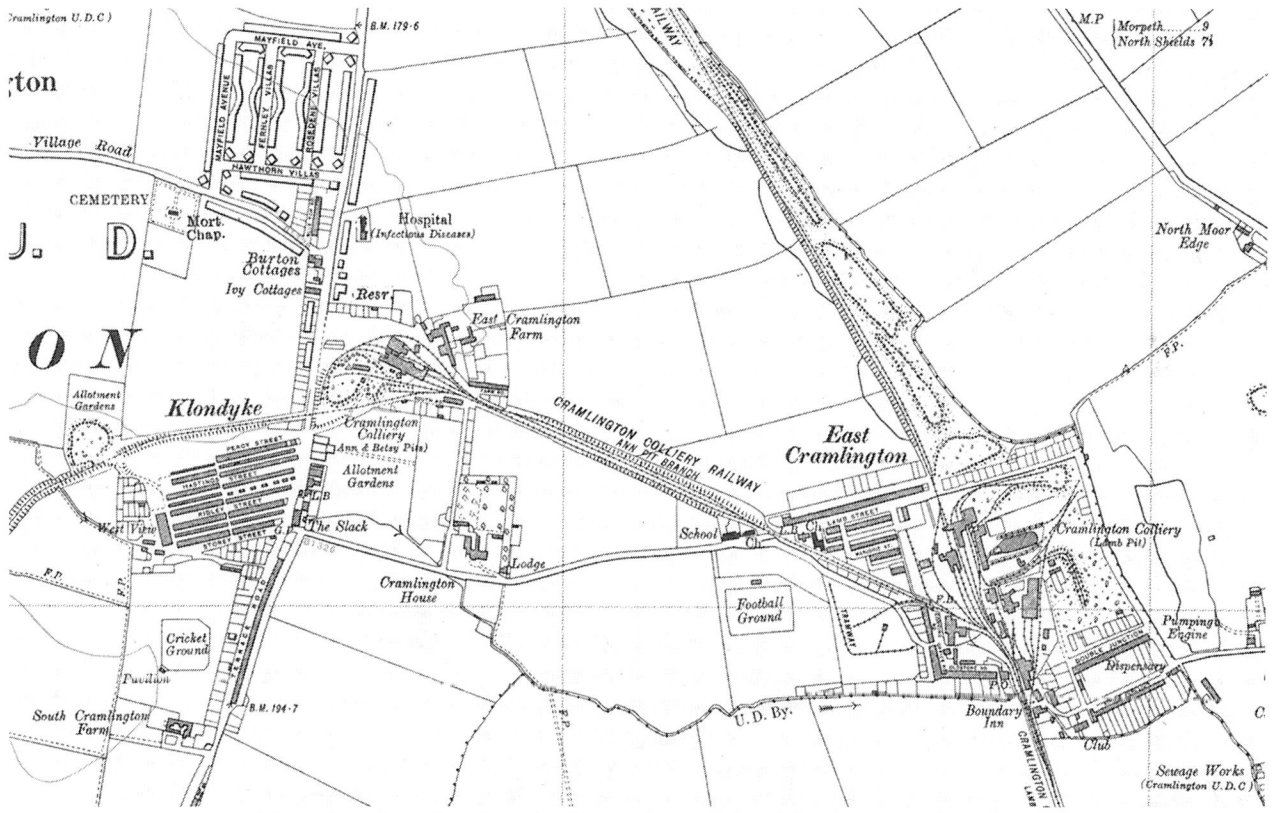

Map showing the Ann & Betsy pits at Klondyke in more detail.[34]

Ann Pit, Klondyke, Cramlington.

---

[32] Named Ann after Joseph Lamb's mother.

[33] It is not known whether this is the date when the sinking commenced; when it was completed; or when the first coal was extracted. Durham Mining Museum http://www.dmm.org.uk/colliery/c040.htm.

[34] O.S. 4th edition map reproduced with permission of Northumberland Archives.

A petrol locomotive for hauling tubs from West Cramlington to Ann Pit screens.

The 'Betsy' Pit was situated within the same complex at approximately the same distance from the village centre. Work on sinking the shaft at the Betsy began on 19th April 1854. The pit began production in 1856 and its workforce accessed winnable coal in the High Main seam, in the 3 feet Beaumont Main seam and in the Brockwell seam of 2 feet 9 inches at 896 feet. Deeper again, at 1086 feet, was another workable seam. At their prime in 1914, the Ann and Betsy Pits employed 451 men and boys underground and 142 on the surface.

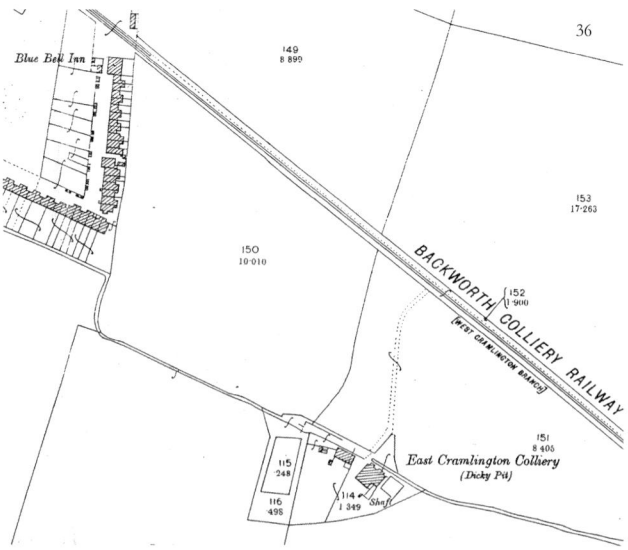

The Dicky Pit, or more correctly the East Cramlington Colliery was owned by Joseph Lamb and Partners and situated about 400 yards south east of West Cramlington Colliery. The pit was situated south of the West Cramlington wagon-way and due west of The Doctor Syntax Inn (later called The Bay Horse) which is adjacent to the Newcastle Road between Annitsford to Klondyke. The Dicky Pit shaft was sunk on 16th November 1849 to a depth of 565 feet. It 'won' coal principally from the Yard, Bensham, Hartley, Low Main and Beaumont seams at between 144 and 565 feet. From March 1932, the Ann Pit was connected underground to the Dicky Pit and by then, more economic output from the Dicky Pit was being acheived.[37]

---

[35] Used with permission of Durham Mining Museum.
[36] O.S. 2nd edition 1897 map reproduced with permission of Northumberland Archives.
[37] *Colliery Engineering*, March 1932, The Hartley Main Collieries Limited, http://www.dmm.org.uk/colleng/3023-01.htm.

Outside the Dicky Pit.

The Amelia[38] Pit's shaft was sunk on 22nd August, 1847 to a depth of 557 feet. This colliery was at Shankhouse, north east of the village centre.[39]

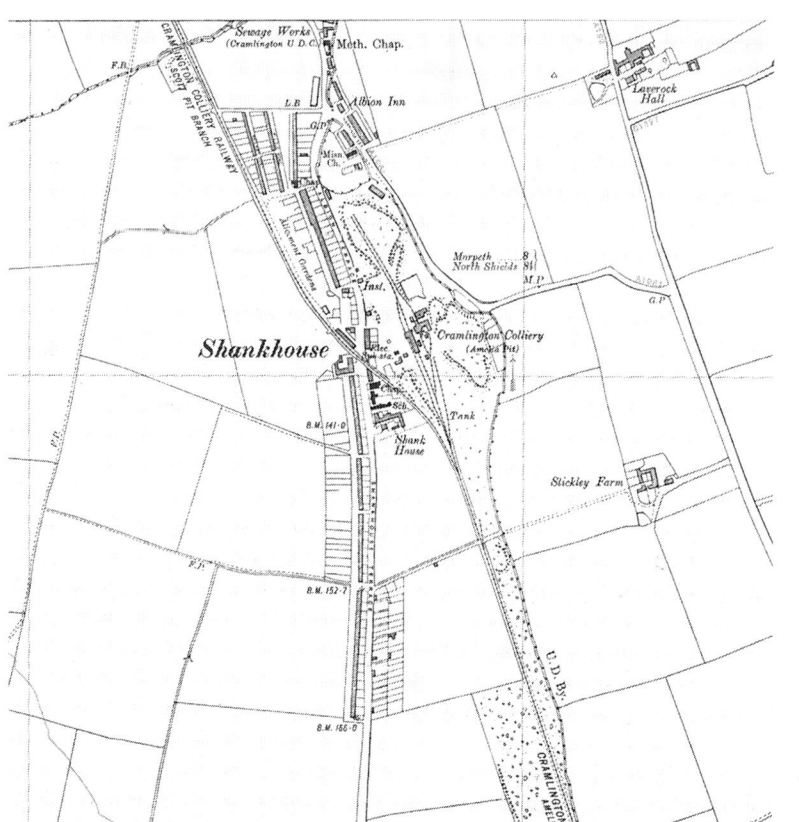

The seams worked there were the High Main seam at 54 feet and the Low Main seam at 482 feet. These seams were respectively 6 feet and 7 feet 5inches thick. Water seepage was a problem and required twenty, 60 gallon tubs per hour to shift it from the high seam.

---

[38] The Amelia Pit was named after Amelia Lamb, the wife of the owner, Joseph Lamb.
[39] East of Amelia Pit at Shankhouse, towards Stickley Farm there was an earlier pit called 'The Joy'.
[40] O.S. 4th edition map reproduced with permission of Northumberland Archives.

Amelia Pit, Shankhouse.

At its most productive, Amelia Pit had a workforce of 673 men and boys, including 256 hewers of coal. The pit also retained six horses and 79 pit ponies.

The belt sheds/coal screens and workmen at the Amelia Pit, Shankhouse, c.1900.

In 1882 an Overman's wage at the Amelia pit was 41 shillings with two shillings extra paid for attendance at the manager's office on a Sunday. A coal hewer earned five shillings and four pence per day, less a charge for gun powder. The trapper boys, usually the boys straight from school, who opened the air-circulation doors to let tubs pass, earned one shilling a day; and the caller or 'knocker-up' received seven shillings a week from the workmen.[41]

---

[41] From an anonymous, handwritten account entitled *Cramlington and Coal* provided by Cramlington Yesterday Society. In 1930 one shilling was worth £2.83p.

Outside the winder-man's cabin at Amelia Pit, *c*.1900, with winder-man R. Tunney on the extreme left.

West Cramlington Colliery was located half a mile south of St. Nicholas Church in the village[43] and employed 130 men and boys, 95 of them coal hewers. Its daily output was 400 tons.

'The original pit at West Cramlington was called the 'Lizzie.' After the closing of the 'Lizzie', the Wrightson Colliery was the means of livelihood. It was always called West Colliery.' [44]

---

[42] Image provided by Betty Norris.
[43] West Cramlington Colliery was where present day (2014) Alexandra Park is located.
[44] Hancock, Thomas, *Unpublished History of the Hancock Family of Cramlington* (Nov 1983) p.5.

The name 'Wrightson' is believed to relate to the mining equipment of that name used at the pit.

In an article written by John Brownlee for *The Sunday Sun* newspaper published on 14th December 1958, Jack Wilson, who started at Shankhouse when he was 12 and rose to become under-manager of West Cramlington Colliery, is quoted as saying: *'the Wrightson pit … was originally called the Queen Pit when it opened after Queen Victoria. We were producing about 500 tons of good grade coal daily. (We had) … about 178 hand hewers and about 30 shifters. Many of us thought this could have continued if the pit had been properly worked. But the new management were taking coal out from anywhere they could get it … even the sides of the roadways.'*

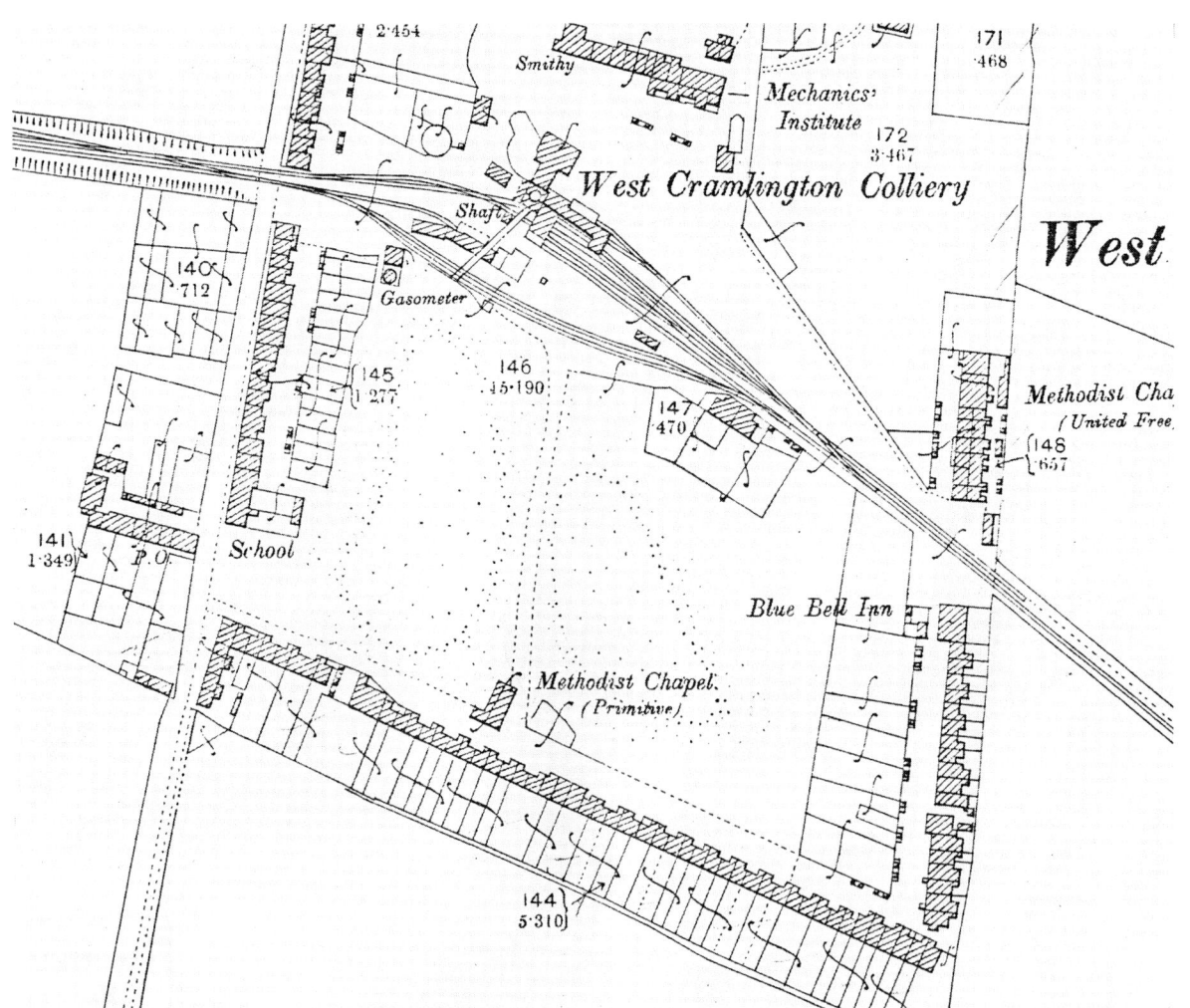

The colliery shaft was within the elliptically shaped limits of the rail track. It was close to Bell's Farm and Bell's Cottages. The pit heap occupied much of the inside of the rectangular village and between the heaps ran 'black road' and 'gassy gutter'; a stagnant stream which carried residue for the mine and gas works before disappearing underground near Cross Row. Above the colliery buildings were the smithy's building and on the opposite end of the short row, the Mechanic's Institute which was above the stables and accessed by a ladder. There were two chapels in the village: Primitive and Methodist (known locally as 'Absalom's'[46] and 'Harbottle's'.[47] The Primitive Methodist Chapel was positioned in front of Cross Row, midway along the row. The two chapels were built in 1850 under the guidance and sponsorship of four men; both Lamb brothers, John Straker and Edward Potter, who later became

---

[45] 1897 O.S. map ref 80.12 reproduced with permission of Northumberland Archives.

[46] The Rev Henry Gregory Absalom was laid to rest in St. Nicholas Churchyard on 27th March 1935, aged 64. His wife Ann Hannah was buried there too on 24th March 1946.

[47] The Minister of this chapel was Jack Harbottle who was winder-man at West Cramlington Colliery and a lay-preacher.

Mayor of Tynemouth.[48] William Mitchell's wife ran the little general dealer's shop which sold everything from paraffin and carbide to porridge oats. Mr. Jack Wilson is reported to have said: *'In the General Strike ... every family had the same amount of provisions. They always had no more, no less without payment while the strike lasted. It was that sort of community, where troubles were shared.'* [49]

The Blue Bell Inn, seen here on the right *c.*1930, was situated midway between two duck ponds and was surrounded by farm buildings. It was known locally as 'The Box Eggs'. Bill Muckle in his *'No Regrets'* (Newcastle, People's Publications, 1981) p.11, thought the name derives from the licensee refusing credit to a regular customer. In anger the customer accused the licensee of being the opposite of 'a good egg' – as being a 'bloody boxed egg'. Eggs had only recently been offered for sale in boxes. They were cheaper than fresh eggs but often the box contained rotten ones. The nick-name stuck. An alternative explanation was provided by Alan Lowther in a presentation made to Cramlington Yesterday Society on 24th September 1970. Drawing on an article written by George Stephenson in the *Blyth News*, dated 5th December 1968, he stated that the greengrocer started delivering eggs in boxes and men at the Blue Bell, who often took Monday off work, griddled many eggs on an open fire at the pub – and the name 'box egg' stuck. Apparently, in the context of nick-names, there was a house in Blue Bell Row which was known locally as 'Rhubarb Castle'. This was because it was a three storey building of flats, which stood out proud of the other buildings like sprouting rhubarb in a vegetable garden.

In addition to the Blue Bell Inn, which was on the end of Blue Bell Row, West Cramlington had The Doctor Syntax Inn[50] (later the Bay Horse) which was only a few hundred yards away. It also had three grocers, two butchers, a brick and tile manufacturer, (on the land which later became Tilery Farm) a shoe maker, two smiths, three colliery officials, a draper and a school master and mistress. Houses for the mine workers included Lane Row at the western end of the village. The school was at the southern corner of this row. The longest row was called Cross Row and this ran east to west and faced the mine.

West Cramlington Colliery prior to demolition.

---

[48] Taylor, H.A., Cramlington – Historical Survey, (Newcastle, County Hall, July 1963) p.4.

[49] Brownlee, John, *The Sunday Sun* – 14th December, 1958 – The Tragedy When a Pit Village Dies.

[50] A race horse called Doctor Syntax won The Preston Gold Cup seven times, The Richmand Gold Cup five time and The Lancaster Gold Cup five times between 1811 and 1838. Many public houses were named after this horse.

The reporter from the *Newcastle Daily Chronicle* put his own, sometimes erroneous, spin on what he saw in this part of Cramlington: *'Sneakeys Row … (had) the best houses in Cramlington, which only favoured certain individuals, in the five rows, i.e. fathers who had given pledges to society in the shape of a family of strapping sons who will develop sufficient quality of bone and muscle, to make great hewers. The houses though are provided neither with privies nor ash pits and the stench from them together with the smoke from the sulphurous pit heap make a formidable series of drawbacks.'* [51]

Sneaky Row comprised the first few houses in Cross Row and the last houses on Lane Road; so called Sneaky because they were occupied by colliery officials with overseeing responsibilities even outside the mine.

There was a small block of wooden houses called 'Barracks', which were occupied by non-pit workers.[53]

The winding wheels from Wrightson Colliery.[59]

---

[51] *Newcastle Daily Chronicle*, 9th August 1873, p.2.
[52] From Mrs. E. Potts' archive *c.*1956.

[53] None of the houses built during the New Town development were on the site of West Cramlington. The mining village comprising housing, colliery offices and pit heaps now form Alexandra Park.
[59] Image from Susan Napier's collection.

Annie Green in 1938 at West Cramlington Colliery, with the pit heaps behind. Annie died of rheumatic fever, aged 12 years, shortly after this photograph was taken. Image provided by Mr. Dennis Green.

Lamb Pit

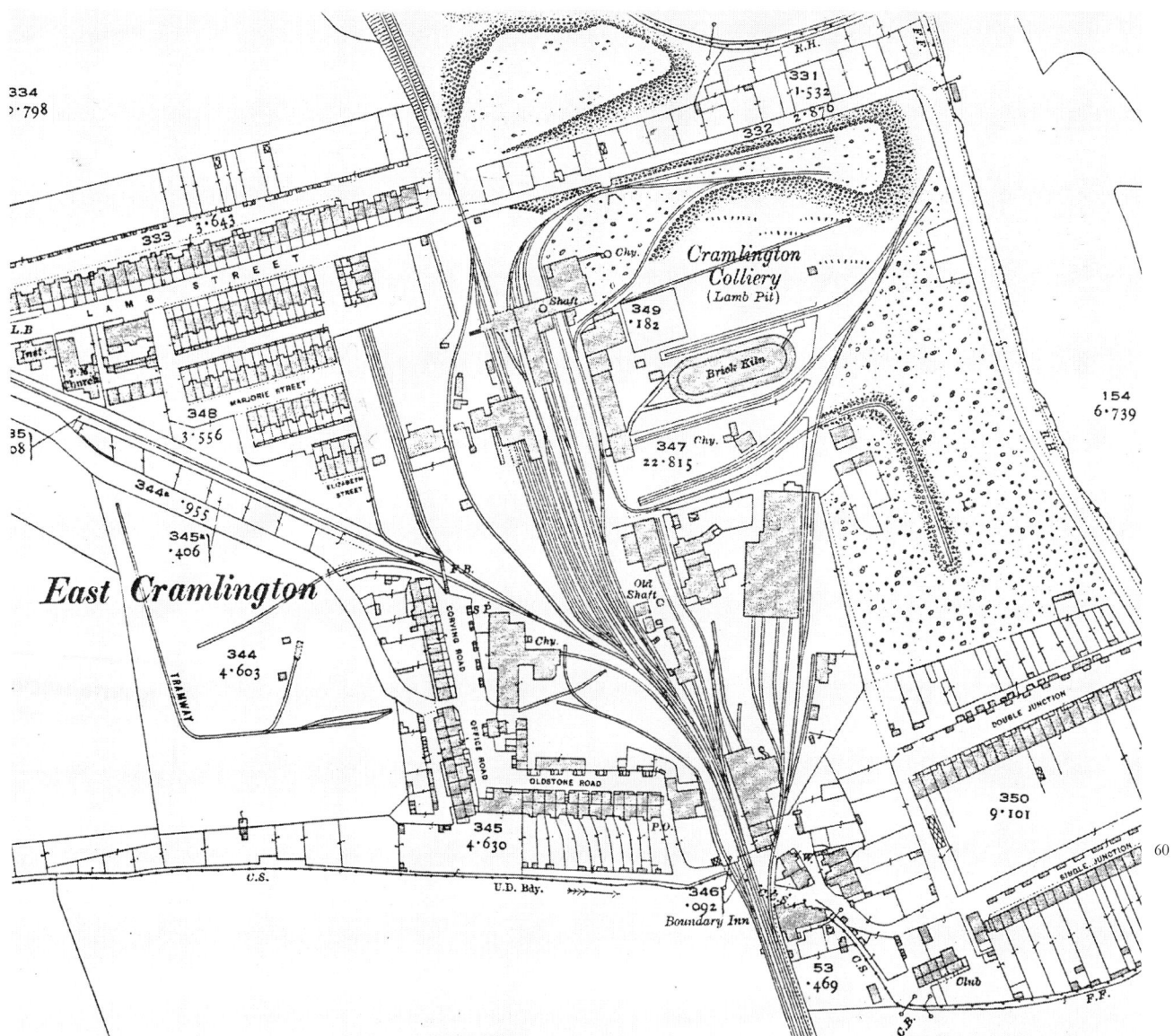

The sinking of the Lamb Pit at East Cramlington began on 16th November 1849. The shaft was almost adjacent to the roadway to the west of the brick kiln. An old shaft is shown to the right of the ten track rail network. The Boundary Inn is shown at the bottom of the map, and at the top left is the United Methodist Chapel. Cropped off the map, left of the chapel was the school,

The mine went to a depth of 367 feet. The colliery worked the Main Five Quarter seam of just over 6 feet and the Yard seam at 338 feet. In 1902, Lamb Pit employed 683 men and boys underground and 304 on the surface. By 1935, when it still had a combined workforce of 526 men and boys, coal production at the Lamb Pit ceased. Fifty two men were retained to work the pumps and coal 'washery 'until 1954.

Houses for the workforce at the Lamb Pit were close to the colliery. Three of the rows were named after the owner and his family: Lamb Street, Marjorie Street and Elizabeth Street. As can be seen, the properties were situated between the mineral line running south west from the Ann and Betsy Pits, and the line operating north south from the Amelia Pit at Shankhouse.

---

[60] O.S. map 1922 reproduced with permission of Northumberland Archives.

Lamb Pit, East Cramlington.

Coal belts and loading jibs at Lamb Pit, *c.*1930.

East Hartford Colliery

Strictly speaking East Hartford Colliery was fractionally outside the boundary of Cramlington Parish. But the workforce for East Hartford and Shankhouse lived cheek by jowl. There was also a sharing of some coal seams underground.

East Hartford Colliery from the south.

Nelson Colliery

Until the 1880s the Ann and Betsy Pits were owned by Joseph Lamb and his partners, but in 1910 they became part of the Cramlington Coal Company.

On 17th December, 1920 the directors of the Cramlington Coal Company were presented with a comprehensive report outlining the proposal to convert and extend the buildings of the Cramlington Airship (see later) into dwelling houses or cubicles for single men working in the mines. The proposal was to provide fittings and appliances, similar to facilities available under Army or Admiralty conditions, for over 200 men. A manager was to be appointed, along with two cooks, four kitchen maids, six waitresses and two porters. The charge to the occupants for renting a 'room' was set at seven shillings per week. Subsequently, the scheme was adopted and single men came into the area to supplement the workforce. By May 1929 the group of Cramlington collieries had been amalgamated with The Seaton Delaval Coal Company to form Hartley Main Collieries Limited.

Towards the end of 1930 Mr. C.A. Nielson,[61] a well-known mining engineer was appointed chairman and managing director of the Hartley Main Company. Aided by Mr. J. A. Metcalf, who was chief engineer, he initiated a policy of modernisation. This involved the electrification of all of their pits, including Hartford, Shankhouse, Cramlington Ann, West Cramlington and the other collieries within the group (Dudley, New Delaval, Seaton Delaval and Hartley). The new coal company sunk their final mine shaft in 1934 at Old Crow Hall Lane, in Cramlington, to a depth of 360 feet to reach the Plessey seam.

Nelson Village, named after the managing director, was constructed in the form of a triangle close to the mine. Building work commenced in the early 1930s, but during the financial depression work stopped and the properties were left in their unfinished state from 1936–1938. The original dwellings were Burdon Avenue, Ross Grove, Chichester Avenue, Rose Avenue, Scott Avenue and Nelson Avenue. Arcot Avenue and Blagdon Crescent were added in 1938 at which time flush toilets were installed in the properties.

Nelson Village houses under the shadow of the airship hangar, *c*.1948.

---

[61] This name was anglicised to Nelson to save any misunderstanding or difficulty following European hostilities.
[62] Image from Susan Napier's collection.

Sammy Brown (postmaster) outside Woodhouse's shop (Airship Cottage), Nelson Village.

'... Nelson Colliery was what many miners would describe as a 'Blackin' Factory', meaning it was small and backward. ... It was worked by hand methods, the transport of coal and materials being by pit pony. The (surface) coal was transported by an endless rope haulage system to the screens at Shankhouse, a distance of little over a mile.' [64]

In 1935 the colliery employed 210 men, 147 of them underground. In 1957 the total number was 258, with 63 of these working on the surface. The low Main seam at Nelson Colliery was abandoned in 1950 and the colliery closed altogether in 1958.

Nelson Colliery, 1935.

---

[63] Image from Susan Napier's collection.

[64] Tuck, James T., *The Collieries of Northumberland Vol. 1*, (Newcastle, Trade Union Press Services, 1993) p.74. Mr. Tuck was writing from the perspective of one who had experienced mining in more enlightened and mechanised times; although the description given was repeated by Mr. Dennis Green who worked at Nelson Colliery.

Nelson Colliery's waste heaps viewed from Crowhall Lane.

[65] Images from Susan Napier's collection.

Arcot Colliery

Alan Hedley, in his book *Arcot Hall – The First 100 Years* reports that *'Several shafts and drifts have been identified close to Arcot, particularly drifts near Arcot House and close to Dudley Lane towards the bend at Dam Dykes. There were mine shafts marginally south and east of the main entrance to the house, with another beyond the small burn which runs north of the Arcot Estate. Coal was extracted using board and pillar processes from the Main, Yard, Maudlin, Low Main and Brass-Thill seams. In places the main seam was eight feet thick and only 28 feet beneath the surface. The Low Seam was up to five feet thick.*

Hartley Main Colliery Limited was responsible for sinking shafts for Arcot at the start of the Second World War. The principal shaft was at the west end of the present car park of Arcot Hall. The winding house remained standing until 1960. Stables for six ponies were located behind the house. 'The horses often came to the surface at the end of each shift.' [66] *A second shaft was sunk north of the house and there was also a ventilation shaft to the west of the house. The mine was worked east of the shafts up to the railway line and coal was taken from the site by wagons entering the west main gate and leaving from the east gate.*

In 1944 Arcot (Drift) Colliery was managed by Mr. H. Taylor and employed 55 men underground and 50 on the surface. In 1945 management had passed to Mr. H. Flesher and he had supervision of 21 underground workmen and 11 on the surface. The colliery stopped production in December 1945.[67]

MINING CONDITIONS

Conditions in the early pits, which had helped develop Cramlington from a mainly agricultural community, improved over time, but as can be seen from the early 20th century images of men waiting to go underground or leaving home at the start of their shift, the workers did not have the advantage of safety helmets or even knee pads, which later became the norm.

---

[66] It is more likely that the horses came to the surface only at the end of their working life or during prolonged periods of stoppage.

[67] Hedley, Alan, *Ibid*, pp.54–57; additional information drawn from Durham Mining Museum indices.

Prior to the Seventh Earl of Shaftsbury's Commission in 1840, which looked into mining conditions and employment issues and then recommended to Government, changes in the laws relating to the employment of children in mines, working class children suffered *'a mass of misery, vice, and depravity.'*

Many of the workers were as young as eight and it was frequently young boys who succumbed to life threatening dangers both on the surface and underground.[68]

In 1910, under the name of David Addy, Peter Dodd wrote *Dusty Diamond* a novel based on Cramlington Collieries. The following is an extract: *'Has anyone tried to picture a child of twelve aroused from his sleep, day after day, at four in the morning, his eyes mere slits of flabby tissue through which he can only see the great red halo around the candle that lights his way down stairs to don his pit clothes? Has the imagination ever conjured up the feelings that these cold and clammy garments (pit clothes are always cold and clammy)* [69] *produce on a boy rising from a warm bed, and the pot of coffee, with a milky crust baked on the top, within the kitchen oven, as foundation meal for twelve hours' toil in a coal mine?*

… The pit itself was damp, dark and close,[70] *with water trickling down its cavernous sides; the floor ankle deep in black mud and around, a labyrinth of dark and gruesome passages. Behind each door, used for ventilation purposes, a child was seated in total darkness. It was his duty, on hearing the approach of the 'corve' or coal truck, to pull open the door, to which a string was attached, and shut it immediately the corve had passed. From the time the first coal was brought forward in the early morning until the last corve had passed at night, a period of twelve or fourteen hours, the little trapper, unable to stir more than a dozen paces lest he should neglect his duty, was at his monotonous and deadly work. … spending his days, from five in the morning till five at night, behind a trap door … for a penny an hour. Except on Sunday he never saw the sun. All the circumstances of a little trapper's life were full of horror; and upon nervous and sensitive children, the effect was terrible.'* [71]

---

[68] The Durham Mining Museum's record show that between 1836 and 1934 a total of 259 workers were killed in Cramlington pits. Thirty-five of these were boys aged sixteen or under who lost their lives in the 19th century. Seven were aged twelve or under; one was only eight. Most of these juveniles were crushed by a collapse of stone or run over by wagons. One sixteen year old died in an explosion.
[69] See also W. Muckle, *No Regrets*, (Newcastle, People's Publications, 1981) p.17. *'I've come home from the pit wet to the skin some days and my clothes have not been dry next morning, but they've still had to go on again for another shift. With the money you got then you could not buy more clothes.'*
[70] 'Close', meaning hot, humid and damp.
[71] Dodd, Peter, *Dusty Diamonds*, (Exceter, Besley and Dalgleish, 1910) pp.87 and 90.

Boys with their 'midgy' lamps.[72]

[72] *'Midgy' or 'Midgie' lamps were fueled by oil and had an exposed flame protected only against draught by the outer casing. Such lamps continued to be used in pits which were considered less 'fiery', well into the 20th century* – Atkinson, Frank, *The Great Northern Coalfield 1700–1900*, (Newcastle, Frank Graham, 1979) p.20.

Miners before their shift, *c*.1900

Commonly in the Cramlington pits, there were rotations of three ten or twelve hour shifts, early, back and night; the night shift being maintenance men, shifting stone, propping and preparing road and tram ways for the production shifts. Hewers were piece workers who were paid on the amount of coal they produced. When their working practices became more organised, they moved their place of work at the coal face every three months. Their changed position depended on the drawing of lots or *cavilles* as this process was known.

The coal face could be anything up to four miles from the bottom of the shaft and the workers carried their *'smokies'* or paraffin lamps for light on the way in and out to the face. At the coal face a candle would be used. This was held in a simple wire holder with a spiked bottom to stick into any convenient pit prop. The deputy or shot firer would blast the seam at the face, then the hewer would dig the coal out using a heart-shaped shovel. If it was a thick seam he would sit on a small three-legged stool or *'crackett'*. If it was a low seam, he would lie on his side to draw out the coal before shovelling it into tubs brought by a *'putter'*. If there was an excess of stone or waste in the tubs, the hewers were penalised.

Tom Endean's previously unpublished poem below reflects on a slightly later period, but it has relevance in putting into context the mine worker's contribution to community and to wider society.

'A Miner's Plight' [73]
'My father was a miner, an honest man and just,
He left the mine at 49, a victim of the dust.
They sent him down the hell-hole, a boy of thirteen years,
Coal was cheap and plentiful, and wet with children's tears.

---

[73] From the archives of Cramlington Yesterday Society.

There he lost his boyhood, a man before his time,
God fearing and hard working and spent at forty nine.
Along with fellow miners, he took the blows and kicks,
When the miners were defeated in nineteen twenty six.

Driven back by hunger, to keep the mine and the drift,
And wage that was disgraceful, less then seven bob a shift.
The Master in his Mansion, now had it cut and dried,
Coal was cheap and plentiful and the miners' hands were tied.

But things don't always operate, the way that they are planned.
For fate stepped through the doorway and Kismet took a hand.
Hitler marched on Europe, the Second War began –
And suddenly the miners were heroes to a man.

They kept the engines turning, in that savage six years fight,
And every miner played his part against the German might.
With peace once more upon us, and massive Labour gains,
The Master in his Mansion, no longer held the reins.

We now know of the horror and devastating plight,
Of all the sorry pit-folk, who thought they'd won the fight.
The Unions are in danger, of that there is no doubt,
So fight now for our future, that's what it's all about.'

Richard Fyne expressed a similar idea when he quoted an old poem in his detailed account of the plight of Northumberland and Durham miners:

'Men by labour, men by feeling
Men by thought, and men by fame,
Claiming equal rights to sunshine
In man's ennobling name.' [74]

By 1887 the Ann Pit employed 592 men and boys, and like the Amelia Pit, with 673 males, yielded about 700 tons of coal each ten hour day. The West Pit employed 130 men and yet the output there was 400 tons a day. By 1889 the daily combined output of Cramlington Coal Company was 3,000 tons.

Regional production of coal in 1860 was 19 million tons. In 1880 it was 35 million tons and way up to 55 million in 1910. The number of miners in the region rose from 40,000 in 1850 to 215,000 in 1910. However, bad planning did not increase the welfare or working conditions of the workforce. Miners banded together in Unions to try to improve conditions and to break the agreement whereby men bonded to work for the same mine owner for one year without the employer being obliged to give any security of tenure during the same period. Union efforts to secure better working conditions and increased wages were unsuccessful. Union efforts were hampered by workers coming from other areas, particularly Ireland where famine conditions were prevalent and Scotland where farm workers existed like bondsmen. Others came from the lead mines of Durham. Later large numbers came from Cornwall following the market recession for tin, due to it being imported cheaply from the Far East.

When the East Cramlington 'colliery's fell into disuse the nearest seat of operations was at High Pit, half a mile to the west. Here … are the company and repair shops with eight locomotives, stationary wagons and tubs, which are continually in need of some cobbling. There are saw mills and vertical frame saws, propelled by lungs of boiler plates inflated by fiery steam with the power of 100 sawyers.

---

[74] Fynes, Richard, *The Miners of Northumberland and Durham* (Sunderland, Thomas Summerbell, 1873) p.284.

There is a Reading Room for its 154 members … tables well supplied with newspapers … but the smell from the neighbouring gas works pervades the room.' [75]

Tommy Dickson prior to going to the pit in 1935.[76]

---

[75] *Newcastle Daily Chronicle*, 2nd August 1873, p.2.
[76] Image from Laura Hancock's collection.

FATALITIES IN CRAMLINGTON COLLIERIES

Surname	Forename	Date of Event	Age	Cause
Abbott	Christopher	12/07/1905	22	Crushed by locomotive.
Alexander	William	24/04/1885	14	Run over by wagons.
Allan	J.	20/09/1940	57	Crushed by fall of stone.
Allen	Robert	31/10/1867	45	Fell down shaft.
Appleby	John Thomas	05/08/1936	44	Crushed by fall of stone.
Armstrong	James	05/04/1859	71	Run over by tubs.
Armstrong	William Robert	29/04/1904	20	Run over by train.
Baker	William	14/08/1853	33	Gas explosion.
Barlow	James	12/05/1866	10	
Barrass	John	03/10/1857	44	Fell down shaft.
Batey	Robert	20/03/1900	48	Fell from nine feet platform.
Baxter	James	04/08/1841	10	Run over by tubs.
Beecher	Edward	18/01/1867	29	Crushed by roof collapse.
Bell	Thomas	30/06/1842	23	Crushed by fall of stone.
Bennett	Joseph	20/09/1838	41	Crushed by fall of stone.
Brannangan	James	30/09/1888	42	Crushed by fall of stone.
Brooks	John	14/11/1876	45	Crushed by fall of stone.
Brown	John	16/08/1856	31	Crushed by rope.
Brown	Matthew	25/04/1861	35	Crushed by fall of stone.
Brown	Robert	11/03/1849	37	Died following knee injury.
Brown	Robert	27/06/1853	15	Run over by tubs.
Bruce	John	02/03/1842	28	Gas explosion.
Bruce	John	03/05/1920	71	Thrown from cart.
Bruce	Philip	11/09/1905	16	Crushed by tubs.
Bryden	Anthony	15/03/1844	39	Drawn over the pullies.
Bryden	Thomas	10/06/1911	51	Crushed by fall of stone.
Brydon	Thomas	04/11/1931	23	Crushed by fall of stone.
Budge	William Henry	23/11/1905	33	
Burn	William	02/04/1853		
Burrell	John	19/08/1862	52	Crushed by fall of stone.
Carr	Thomas	13/11/1901	50	Fell down shaft.
Carter	William	26/08/1889	15	Crushed by tubs.
Charlton	John	21/11/1854	71	Crushed by wagons.
Chennall	William	22/05/1900	30	Crushed by fall of stone.
Clark	Ernest	01/08/1906	22	
Clough	Henry	20/06/1855	17	Crushed by fall of stone.
Crawford	Andrew	01/09/1918		Died in pit.
Crisp	William	13/02/1891	48	Crushed by fall of stone.
Davidson	James	07/04/1915	17	Crushed by fall of stone.
Davison	Isaac	23/07/1906	37	Crushed by tubs.
Davison	Ralph	22/02/1850	21	Crushed by fall of stone.
Dawson	John	16/03/1836	21	Crushed by fall of stone.
Dawson	William	14/12/1910	48	Crushed by fall of stone.
Diery	Edward	27/10/1906	38	
Diery	Philip Henry	27/10/1906	36	
Diston	George	17/10/1906	50	Crushed by fall of stone.
Dixon	Edward	01/06/1908	24	Crushed by fall of stone.
Dixon	John	06/03/1850	50	Crushed by fall of stone.
Dixon	John	06/07/1871	12	Crushed between tubs.
Dixon	John	13/11/1914	17	Crushed between tubs.
Dixon	Matthew	23/07/1909	14	Crushed between props.
Dobson	Ralph P.	31/07/1937	52	
Dodd	Edward	30/10/1841	21	Crushed by fall of stone.
Dodds	Robert	11/12/1846	14	Crushed by cage.
Donaldson	William Steel	02/07/1888	18	Crushed by roof collapse.
Doney	Luke	07/04/1880	24	Crushed by fall of stone.
Doney	William Thos.	19/03/1906	33	Brain congestion.
Ducker	James	14/02/1928	47	Crushed by fall of stone.
Dumma	William	07/03/1916	23	Crushed by wagons.
Dunn	John	03/01/1884	20	Crushed by fall of stone.
Elliot	Andrew	22/10/1859	36	Tetanus following amputation after being crushed by fall of stone.
Ellison	Thomas	29/12/1884	16	Crushed by tub.
Ellison	William	30/10/1841	37	Crushed by fall of stone.
Endean	Francis	19/12/1929	64	Crushed by fall of stone.

Surname	Forename	Date of Event	Age	Cause
Farthing	Jonathan	06/06/1899	37	Fell down shaft.
Floyd	John	15/08/1901	16	Run over by wagons.
Flynn	L.J.M.	11/11/1925	44	Crushed by fall of stone.
Foley	Daniel	29/04/1904	29	Fell down shaft.
Forster	James	02/04/1853		
Forster	Robert	01/07/1861	13	Run over by tubs.
Forster	Thomas	14/08/1922	46	Crushed by fall of stone.
Forster	William	22/12/1848	16	Crushed by fall of stone.
Gallon	George	18/04/1850	58	Thrown from tramway.
Gardner	Robert	20/12/1872	14	Crushed by wagons.
Giles	George Wm.	05/07/1906	36	Crushed by fall of stone.
Glanvilee	Thomas	30/03/1892	33	Crushed by fall of stone.
Green	Thomas	08/07/1857	10	Crushed by tubs.
Grey	Mark	14/10/1846	23	Crushed by fall of coal.
Halliday	John	03/11/1870	36	Crushed by fall of coal.
Hamilton	George	31/01/1894	17	Crushed by tubs.
Hancock	Samuel	05/12/1908	19	Crushed by tubs.
Hardy	N.	1922		
Hardy	N.	01/06/1942	17	Industrial disease.
Harkinson	William	26/01/1845	15	Crushed by fall of coal.
Harris	James	27/01/1899	36	Crushed by fall of coal.
Harris	John	28/04/1881	30	Crushed by fall of stone.
Harris	John	12/12/1914	46	Fell down.
Hawke	Samuel	15/01/1888	22	Crushed by tubs.
Henderson	Martin	28/05/1857	17	Crushed by fall of stone.
Henderson	William	31/10/1859	49	Explosion.
Henwood	John	02/07/1872	37	Crushed by fall of stone.
Heslop	James	02/04/1890	55	Fell from 'heapstead'.
Heslop	John	25/06/1846	32	Crushed by fall of stone.
Hicks	Edward	17/02/1877	14	Crushed by tubs.
Hicks	John	18/03/1893	38	Crushed by fall of coal.
Hicks	William	27/11/1869	49	Crushed by fall of stone.
Hill	James	16/03/1904	64	'Glanders' horse disease.
Hine	John	07/06/1881	21	Crushed by fall of stone.
Hogg	Cuthbert	15/06/1916	55	Crushed by fall of stone.
Hogg	George	16/01/1846	36	Fell down shaft.
Hogg	William	08/10/1894	46	Crushed by fall of stone.
Holland	Samuel Jeffrey	25/07/1901	38	Crushed by fall of stone.
Hooper	James Thos.	09/06/1911	30	Crushed by fall of stone.
Hooper	Joseph	08/01/1934	45	Crushed by fall of stone.
Hooper	Robert	10/05/1928	43	Crushed by fall of stone.
Howard	William	08/02/1873	21	Explosion.
Hudson	John	20/06/1859	18	Thrown by locomotive.
Isaac	John	09/02/1921	43	Crushed by fall of stone.
Isaacs	James	09/02/1881	27	Crushed by fall of stone.
Jefferson	William	13/11/1855	64	Crushed by fall of stone.
Jeffreys	Thomas	22/07/1859	23	Crushed by fall of stone.
Jobling	Robert	11/10/1845	34	Crushed by cage.
Jobson	Thomas	04/10/1848	28	Explosion.
Jobson	William	02/05/1910	25	Crushed by fall of stone.
Johnson	George	16/08/1898	32	Crushed by hauling engine.
Jordan	James	24/10/1903	29	Crushed by surface train.
Jewitt	John	02/08/1898	59	Crushed by fall of stone.
Kay	John	06/10/1892	48	Crushed by tubs.
Keeler	J.	14/12/1866	13	
King	Hugh	17/03/1892	36	Crushed by tubs.
Knight	William	14/04/1892	17	Crushed by tubs.
Laidler	Joseph	11/05/1907	18	
Lamonby	Edward	11/01/1898	22	Head injury.
Lashbrook	William	11/07/1898	68	Collapse in pit.
Laverick	James	14/08/1853	48	Explosion.
Leightley	Anthony B.	13/07/1904	39	Heart disease
Lemain	Henry	08/02/1873	15	Crushed by tubs.
Lemin	Edward	21/12/1919	39	Crushed by fall of coal.

Surname	Forename	Date of Event	Age	Cause
Lenton	John	15/03/1844	47	Drawn over the pullies.
Loader	William	14/12/1897	53	Crushed by fall of stone.
Locke	Charles	14/08/1871	18	
Lockyer	A.E.	1918		
Longstaff	Leonard C.	15/04/1911	17	Crushed by tubs.
Mack	William	06/07/1842	26	Crushed by fall of stone.
Masters	William Henry	17/10/1868	20	Crushed by fall of stone.
Matthews	George	22/06/1893	32	Crushed by fall of stone.
McCourt	Patrick	06/08/1877	26	Crushed by fall of roof.
McGuiness	Thomas	27/09/1872	58	Crushed by tubs.
McKenzie	William	06/01/1879	55	Crushed by tubs.
McNully	Hugh	25/04/1885	51	Crushed by truck.
Metcalf	Thomas	08/08/1858	13	Explosion.
Metcalf	Joseph	18/03/1880	29	Crushed by fall of stone.
Milburn	James	09/07/1840	8	Run over by 'rollies'.
Milburn	Thomas	23/03/1860	24	Caught by wagon.
Mitcheson	G.R.	26/05/1894	14	Run over by tubs.
Morrell	John	23/03/1900	16	Crushed by wagons.
Morrison	George Wm.	23/10/1925	27	Crushed by fall of stone.
Mortimer	James	24/01/1871	37	Crushed by fall of stone.
Moss	George	27/09/1867	49	Crushed by fall of stone.
Murphy	Thomas	10/10/1844	22	Falling from 'loop'.
Mutton	James Henry	05/06/1890	40	Crushed by fall of coal.
Narey	Patrick	12/11/1912	25	Scalded.
Nelind	Thomas	11/12/1890	23	Crushed by fall of stone.
Nesbit	James	12/10/1841	49	Explosion.
Nesbit	John	30/10/1841	23	Crushed by fall of stone.
Nesbitt	William	20/10/1908	59	Heart failure – bad air.
Nicholson	George	03/10/1848	40	Explosion.
Oswald	William	29/10/1842	16	Run over by 'rollies'.
Oxenham	William	28/08/1874	32	Crushed by fall of stone.
Parry	John	17/09/1844	22	Crushed by fall of stone.
Patterson	George Laing	10/12/1915	31	Run over by wagons.
Pedrick	William	14/02/1867	44	Crushed by fall of stone.
Philips	John Joseph	25/06/1918	22	Crushed by wagons.
Phillips	William	22/04/1842	32	Run over by wagons.
Pile	Richard	12/09/1851	47	Crushed by tubs.
Porteus	Ronald	28/09/1886	64	Crushed by fall of stone.
Potter	George	03/07/1842	16	Crushed by fall of stone.
Potts	Thomas	11/08/1845	30	Fell down shaft.
Pringle	Robert	23/10/1912	66	
Redstone	James	11/05/1869	19	Crushed by fall of stone.
Reed	William Henry	21/03/1904	33	
Reynolds	William	09/10/1884	60	Crushed by fall of stone.
Richardson	Alexander	30/08/1898	63	Crushed by tubs.
Richardson	Robert	07/07/1847	14	Crushed by cage.
Ridley	Matthew	23/10/1893	22	Crushed by wagons.
Ritson	Anthony	14/11/1854	45	Explosion.
Ritson	William	21/08/1888	45	Crushed by tubs.
Roberts	Henry	22/09/188?	13	Crushed by tubs.
Roberts	James	14/10/1869	58	Crushed by tubs.
Roberts	Thomas	09/10/1866	18	Run over by wagons.
Roberts	Thomas	09/10/1867	8	Run over by wagons.
Robinson	Thomas Jas.	25/05/1907	47	
Robinson	William	16/07/1868	30	Crushed by fall of stone.
Ross	George	28/11/1855	31	Crushed by fall of stone.
Ross	John	19/07/1928	19	Caught by fork shaft.
Sanders	Evan	22/04/1869	64	Crushed by tubs.
Scott	John	24/06/1846	30	Fell down shaft.
Scott	John	20/10/1846	30	Run over by tubs.
Settery	George	19/01/1930	62	Crushed by fall of stone.
Shield	Edward	14/10/1869	34	Explosion.
Shields	George	24/06/1846		Fell down shaft.
Slade	Robert	19/07/1892	55	

Surname	Forename	Date of Event	Age	Cause
Smith	James	07/08/1877	15	Crushed by coal wagons.
Smithson	Joseph	21/02/1892	21	
Stanton	H.	05/10/1916	57	Crushed by fall of stone.
Stark	Richard	28/11/1890	25	Crushed by fall of stone.
Station	James	1897	58	Died in pit.
Stead	John	19/09/1887	14	Crushed by tubs.
Stephens	Thomas	09/12/1898	17	Crushed by tubs.
Stephenson	George	28/09/1886	32	Crushed by fall of stone.
Strong	Robert	26/01/1887	56	Crushed by fall of stone.
Thompson	William	18/05/1883	68	Struck by rope chain.
Todd	George	18/05/1883	13	Crushed by surface wagons.
Todd	James	28/04/1932	59	Explosion.
Trafford	Isaac	06/05/1905	32	Crushed by fall of stone.
Trevethick	Stephen	17/10/1871	29	Crushed by fall of stone.
Trudgeon	John	23/03/1867	36	Crushed by fall of stone.
Turnbull	Robert	07/09/1892	14	Blood poisoning following injury to the leg.
Turnbull	Thomas	16/06/1893	58	Bled to death following injury to head.
Turbull	William	06/12/1897	58	Died in pit.
Tyrell	Richard	06/12/1892	40	Crushed by stone.
Urwin	James	21/09/1868	19	Crushed by fall of stone.
Voisey	William	21/05/1873	19	Crushed by fall of stone.
Voisey	William	21/07/1881	66	Crushed by fall of stone.
Walker	Edward Henry	10/11/1886	15	Crushed by fall of stone.
Walker	John	17/03/1886	62	Crushed by fall of stone.
Walker	William	20/10/1904	22	
Walsall	Samuel	07/10/1892	39	Crushed by fall of stone.
Walsh	Patrick	30/04/1892	54	Crushed by fall of stone.
Wardale	George	13/12/1893		Run over by train.
Watson	John	26/08/1897	30	Crushed by fall of stone.
Watson	Joseph	06/12/1838	51	Crushed by fall of stone.
Waugh	Edward	15/07/1912	33	Septic wound.
Weaver	Albert	/04/04/1870	11	Fall while signalling.
Weaver	William	28/12/1867	37	Crushed by tubs.
Wheatley	Joseph	30/03/1908	65	Crushed by fall of stone.
Wilkinson	George	22/03/1857	50	Crushed by wagon.
Williamson	Frederick	22/09/1857	50	Septic wound.
Willis	William R.	29/02/1904	55	
Wilson	James	1926		
Wilson	Michael	23/01/1892	38	Crushed by fall of stone.
Wilson	Thomas	22/09/1858	41	Hit by wood falling down shaft.
Wilson	William	08/07/1893		Crushed by falling stone.
Wilson/Oatman	James	29/11/1925	43	Killed on surface.
Wonnacot	William	21/03/1904	46	
Wonnacot	John Jeffrey	10/04/1905	58	Crushed by fall of stone.
Wood	James Henry	??/11/1915	48	
Wood	William	10/05/1862	13	Crushed by tubs.
Woolfries	Robert	01/04/1884	15	Crushed by tubs.
Worthley	William	20/01/1866	37	Crushed by fall of stone.
Wright	George	22/08/1932	62	
Wright	James	15/03/1870	14	Crushed by cage.
Wrightson	Charles	23/08/1906	64	
Young	Angus	14/01/1909	21	Crushed by fall of stone.
Young	Joseph	13/08/1841	52	Crushed by fall of stone.
Younger	John	28/08/1892	61	Crushed by fall of stone.

EAST CRAMLINGTON BRICKWORKS

East Cramlington Brickworks was opened in 1896 adjacent to the Lamb Pit at East Cramlington. Jack Raffle, who took many of the photographs included in this book was a long time employee of the Brickworks. Three other former employees, Jim Burridge, Norman Bell and Norman Massey provided a written outline of its history and how the physical building blocks of community were made.

In 1909 a 14 chamber Hoffman continuous kiln was built beside the Lamb Pit by the colliery masons employed by Cramlington Coal Company. There were no partition walls inside the kiln. Bell dampers were raised or lowered on lever screw rods placed on top of the kiln. These dampers controlled the gases leaving the kiln via a main flue which ran through the centre of the kiln right up to early 1981 when the brickworks closed. During the early stage of burning, an accelerator drew the steam out of the kiln. An electric fan assisted the 25 feet high flue chimney in extracting the waste gases. An average of 30,000 bricks were drawn from the kiln each day, to give a weekly output of 150,000 bricks.

Prior to the First World War the yard produced a white facing brick made from seggar (fireclay) in the Wrightson mine. The pressed bricks were marked CRAMLINGTON and CRAMTON. In the 1930s and 40s a poorer quality seggar, mainly from the Hartford mine, produced mostly red, common bricks which were marked HMC for Hartley Main Collieries. During the 1960s clay from Acorn Bank and Ewart open cast sites made into red facing bricks, marked NORTHERN for the National Coal Board's Northern Brick Company.

The brickworks had two grinding pans, ten and eleven feet in diameter together with two riddles. A nine feet diameter grinding pan was also used when the yard had an over-lapping four shift per day system in the late 1940s.

Two Bradley and Craven tin press machines made up to 36,000 bricks in an eight hour shift. Up to the Second World War a wire cut machine also made bricks and field drainage pipes. The extruded bricks and pipes and hand rusticated bricks, and specials such as bull-noses, plinths and soaps, were dried on steam-heated Flats before being burned. A Tilery press tried for a short while to make rustics.

In 1939 the yard produced a record output of nearly 16 million bricks. Output in 1938 had been 15,160,000 items. In the month of September 1939 the yard supplied 67,000 bricks to the Hartley Man group of collieries i.e. the Nelson, Lamb, Dudley, Hartley, Hartfod and Shankhouse mines, and also 1,068,000 bricks were sold to outside customers and another 163,000 went to build air raid shelters.

In 1946 the machine house was rebuilt after fire had burned the old one down. The brickworks employed 28 men in 1979.'

Staff at East Cramlington Brick Works.[77]

---

[77] The image above and the two following are used with permission of Beamish Museum Archives.

Bradley & Craven brick press with operative.

Bradley & Craven grinding mill with workman T. Bartlett.

HOUSING AND INFRASTRUCTURE

In Cramlington the workmen's homes were situated near the collieries and the travelling journalist from the *Newcastle Daily Chronicle* of 1873 described them as follows:

'Old Stone Row – a single house for three families. They boast one small window which barely suffices to light up its limited area.

Corving Row – feeble wood framed houses making some pretence of comfort on the strength of having 2 rooms on the ground floor.

Special Row – a very sorry affair ... and its name can only be accounted for as if the houses had been constructed for little men with no wife and no children.

Double Wood Row – with distinctive roofs which appear to have been cobbled together for mutual support, as if they were not backed up, they might blow over.

New Stone Row – with the nicest concrete floors and 2 downstairs rooms and 'ceiled' upstairs attics.

Half a mile from these houses are the isolated Slack Row, High Pit Row and Terrace Row, which have the advantage of a turnpike road between them and the pit heaps, and they are sheltered behind a garden paling.'

Near the houses were two chapels; the Primitive Methodist Chapel having been built by Connexion; the United Methodists Free Church was close at hand.' [78]

At the beginning of the 20th century any traveller, following a linear route north on Newcastle Road from St. John the Baptist Roman Catholic Church at Annitsford, would encounter many features which no longer exist. First, on the west side of the road was Foster's motor haulage premises. Next was a straight row of red bricked houses called Sanderson Terrace.[79] Immediately before the colliery wagon-way, which led from West Cramlington Colliery to Seghill, was Hewitt's cart and horse sheds. This was on the east side of the road. A few yards further, on the west side of the road was the Doctor Syntax Public House, which later changed its name to the Bay Horse. Opposite, on the east side were the powder cabin for the colliery, the Methodist Manse and a row of dwellings called Collingwood Buildings. The building at the north end of the row was the Smith family's shop. South Cramlington Farm (sometimes known as Botany Bay) was on the left and situated immediately before the Ann Welfare Ground, where there were both cricket and football pitches. Opposite the 'Welfare', immediately before the junction leading east to the Lamb Pit at East Cramlington and Seaton Delaval, was Terrace Row with 46 dwellings. Here the main road was called Terrace Road. Following the colliery 'Strike', which is discussed in more detail later, Terrace Row became known as Cornish Terrace. Immediately beyond Terrace Row, on the right, was the road to East Cramlington. The houses on the corner, beyond the junction, was the terrace of five houses called Slack Cottages.[80]

From the image on the right, beyond the junction, can be seen the front elevation of the cinema and three shops; hardware, post office and shoe shops owned by the James Family. In the distance is High Pit's waste heap.

---

[78] *Newcastle Daily Chronicle*, Ibid, p.2.

[79] Sanderson Terrace was built in 1876 and the remaining two houses are now used as a pre-school nursery.

[80] Dennis Green thought that Slack Cottages got their name from bus and wagon drivers 'slackening off' their acceleration as they gently went down the small incline into Klondyke. Patrons would ask to be off at 'Slack Corner'.

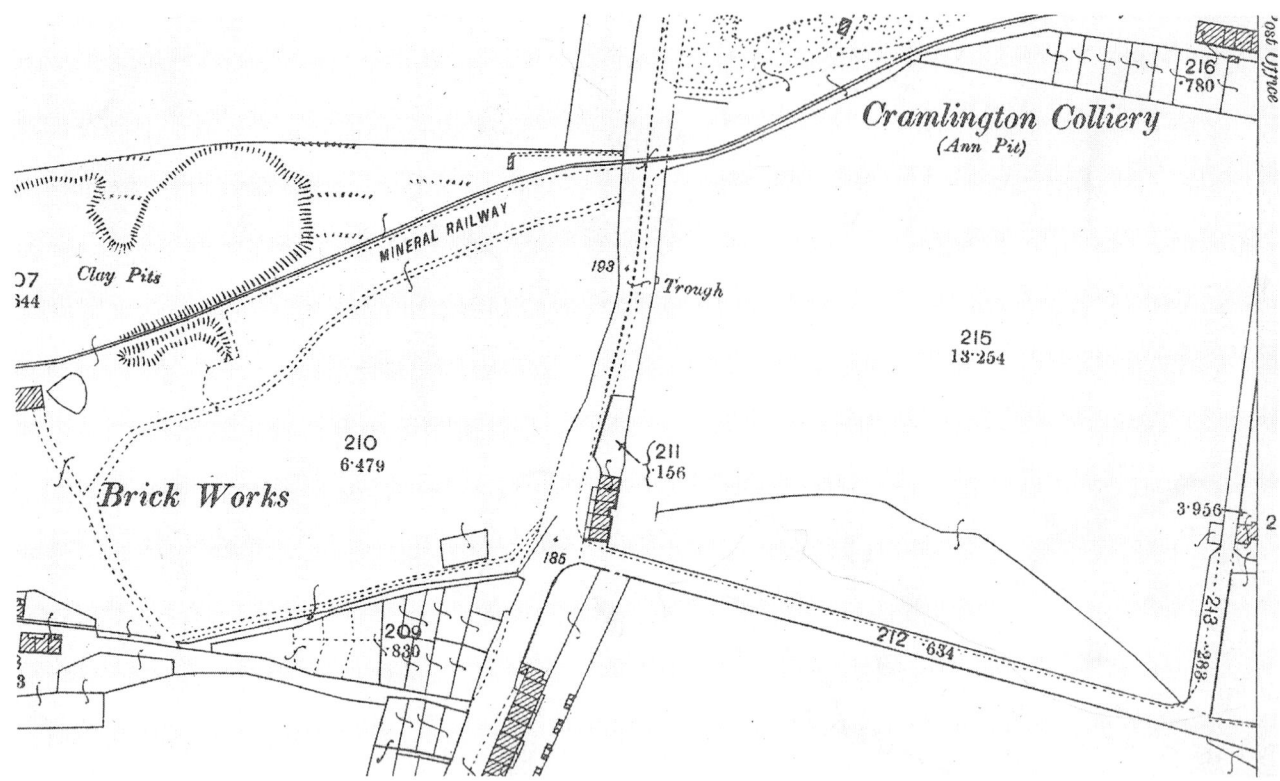

The 1897 map (above)[81] clearly shows the location of Ann Pit (Cramlington Colliery) and the brickyard outline on the left, whereas, by 1922 (below)[82] Klondyke's houses had been built to accommodate workmen employed at the Ann and Betsy Pits.

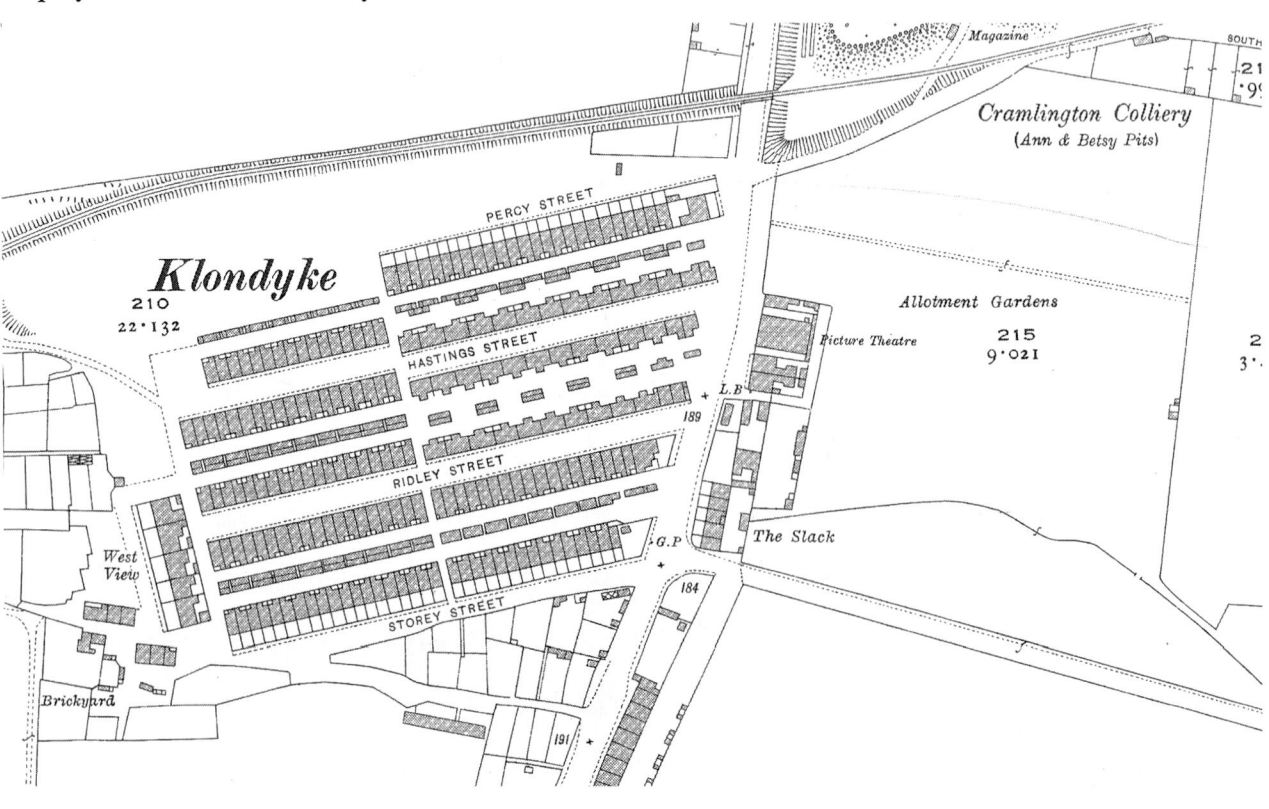

[81] O.S. 25" 2nd edition for 1897 (ref 80.08) reproduced with permission of Northumberland Archives.
[82] O.S. 25" 3rd edition for 1922 (ref 78.13) reproduced with permission of Northumberland Archives.

Continuing along Newcastle Road/Terrace Road, the King George/Rex cinema (right) would have been encountered.

Patrick Brannigan thought '... *the most important building was the 'Picture Hall' where I could read the posters ... and for two pence go to the Saturday matinee and enjoy a silent film.*' [83]

Mr. Leslie Miners, writing in January 1994 about the 'King George', said, '*A pianist accompanied the films. Sometimes a singer or male voice choir entertained before the films were shown.*' [84]

Alan Lowther speaking to the Cramlington Yesterday group on the work of George Stephenson, a reporter for the *Blyth News* and *Ashington Post*, provided a comment from one of George's articles dated 14th August 1969: '*The old village at Klondyke provided Cramlington with its only Picture Hall. In my young days I used to go to this building for a two-penny matinee on a Saturday. It was usually packed to capacity and a swarthy gentleman, sometimes impolite and sometimes downright rude, known as Peters the Manager, walked up and down the aisles shouting threats and even evicting those who failed to obey. At night he would not let the piano player play 'God save the King', if there was the slightest chance of him missing the last bus home to Newcastle.*'

Middle: This alternative view of the picture hall shows also the hardware, shoe and post office shops owned by the James family.

After passing the cinema, there were Bob Lawson's butchers shop and Fenwick Barrass' barber shop, which was on the west side of Newcastle Road. At this point there was a bridge over the road which carried rail traffic from West Cramlington to East Cramlington via High Pit, Betsy and Ann Pits.

---

[83] Brannigan, Patrick, *A Senior Citizen goes to College*, p.3.
[84] From Cramlington Yesterday Society's archive.

As the colliery workforce expanded additional housing was built in 1894 at Klondyke to accommodate 192 families.[85] The houses were diagonally opposite the collieries on a disused field which had previously been the brickyard. The houses and terraced bungalows were in four streets called Storey, Ridley, Hastings and Percy, named respectively after Robert Storey Esq., who had bought the Lawson family's interest in the manor of Cramlington in 1791; landowner Sir Matthew White Ridley; Lord Hastings of Seaton Delaval; and the Duke of Northumberland, Earl Percy.

'The Klondyke houses had a kitchen with a walk-in pantry and a front room downstairs. The back door opened into the yard ... the front door onto a small garden ... towards the West Colliery line. The stairs went up from the back door. They were not enclosed and there was a 'bogey hole' under the stairs.[86] *Upstairs there was an attic with skylight at the back and a good size bedroom at the front with a sash opening window. Across the sandstone and dirt back lane were two out houses; one was wash-house complete with coal burning set pot, a small window and batten door; and the other was an earth closet ... with an oval hole cut into the bare seat ... no wonder that a chamber pot was a recognised article of equipment in each bedroom.'* [87]

Five larger houses, adjacent to the workmen's homes, faced away from the colliery in West View.

Percy Street, Klondyke, *c*.1906.

Klondyke's back rows 1940s.

The large detached house adjacent to the rows is thought to have been occupied by one of the colliery officials. The Klondyke rows were less salubrious.

James' hardware and shoe shops, Klondyke, during different periods.

---

[85] Houses at Klondyke (where there was a 'rush for coal') seem to have been named after the area of Klondike near the Yukon River, Canada, when gold was found in nearby Bonanza Creek in 1896 and gave rise to the Klondike gold rush between 1897–1898 and the establishment of the town of Dawson – which is now reduced to a ghost town.

[86] Actually, 38 of the houses are bungalows.
[87] Hancock, *Ibid*, p.11.

Over-crowding of homes was a perennial problem because families were big and there were large numbers of children. Beyond the Klondyke railway bridge, on the east side of the Newcastle Road were the Betsy and Ann Pits. Here the mineral railway line continued east towards Seaton Delaval via East Cramlington and Lamb Pits. On the west side of the road before the junction leading to Cramlington Village were Pontin's fish shop, the Co-operative Store which opened in 1925, the ten houses of Blue Top Road, 5 Ivy Cottages and the Burton House Public House. On the east side of the Newcastle Road, beyond the pits, were North and South High Pit Roads, with 22 houses; the first High Pit Club; J.B. Aisbett's shop and Sam Hawke's shoe shop. Beyond Aisbett's general store was Cramlington's infectious diseases hospital. On the opposite side of Newcastle Road was where in 1924 'New Town' or Mayfield houses were built. Behind the network of rail tracks serving Ann and Betsy Pits, to the east, was East Cramlington Farm. Carrying on past the hospital were the houses of Sea View, then open land until reaching the footpath leading from the 104 houses of Shankhouse Terrace. The path began on the east side of the road and led east towards Stickley Farm. On the same side of the road as the long terrace, were Shankhouse Welfare and football ground; and a communal washhouse. Shankhouse Cooperative Store was also there.

[88]

Brierly's shop was opposite Sinclair and Haggie's Garage (now Scott's) before the High Pit Club.

Brierly's Shop.

---

[88] Image from Susan Napier's collection.

William and Grace James outside the back of 48 Shankhouse Terrace, c.1900.

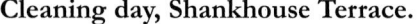

Cleaning day, Shankhouse Terrace.

Part of High Row, Shankhouse Terrace.

The Amelia Pit's labour force lived in houses in Shankhouse Terrace or in the houses opposite or beyond the pit heaps, namely Albion Terrace, Middle Row and Railway Row, the latter of which was next to the colliery mineral line, and in the two rows of Hastings Terrace on either side of the Seaton Delaval road. Some of these houses had brick fronts and wooden backs; others were made completely of wood.

Dinah Tiplady Tunney outside 43 Shankhouse Terrace. [89]

In the late 1940s a hole opened in the road between Albion Terrace and Middle Row, causing significant damage to the houses in that location. The cracks beginning to occur in the stone work (even further south in Shankhouse Terrace) are clear to see. According to Mrs. Irene Keast (née Simpson): *'slippage in these houses became so bad that eventually furniture would slide across the floor as the buildings and foundations started to collapse because of subsidence.'*

Ernest Fletcher Ord, born in Shankhouse in 1895, wrote down his recollections: *'Shankhouse Terrace was the southern part of the village, which was divided by the Coal Company railway which ran between Hartford Coal Mine and Shankhouse, from then on to Lamb Mine.'*

Next to the division caused by the railway line and facing the pit heaps were the Pit Canteen, the Miners' Institute, Labour and Scout huts. The colliery signal cabins were on the south side of the line facing the heaps and the canteen.

---

[89] Image provided by Betty Norris.

Mr. Ord continues: *'The Terrace was divided into four sections, the most southerly one was commonly known as High Row. It was entirely built of stone, whilst the other three were built of red bricks. Each house had a large kitchen, with a door at one side leading out to the front garden. From the kitchen, a passage led to the back door, from then to a small yard which led to the back street. Built on to the passage was a building which was known as the pantry. Sleeping accommodation was provided by having two bedrooms upstairs, but those with large families often had a double bed for the parents in the kitchen.*

As this was the age before electricity, illumination was provided by burning paraffin oil in lamps either standing on the table or hanging from the ceiling. Wooden spouts were provided to run water running from the roof when it rained to a large barrel which stood in the back yard. This was known as the rain-tub. Funnily enough this water was preferred for bathing and washing clothes, to that which was provided by the Council in taps about fifty yards apart.

A big zinc bath ... males and females bathed on a different night on the mat in front of the fire.' [90]

The back door was most commonly used in miners' houses. Indeed, the word 'back' was used all the time.

'After tea, I was allowed to go out to play. Where I lived, I would go through the 'back end' to get to the 'back door' to get to the 'back street.' [91]

Shankhouse houses with Webster's Buildings, the Primitive Chapel to the right of the properties and the school next to it on the right.

On 26th July 1873 the reporter for the *Newcastle Weekly Chronicle* made another one of his visits. He wrote – *'Shankhouse is a straggling village ... nearly a mile long, beginning at Boundary Row and finishing at Shankhouse Row, with 114 houses for the men of Amelia Pit and Hartford Colliery. Boundary Row ... has rather neat but small stone cottages, each containing two rooms and a wash house. The end of the village boasts the only public house in the place, the Albion Inn ... a most respectable looking hostelry. Nearby is the Wesleyan Chapel, a most substantial stone building. Albion Row (more correctly – Albion Terrace) ... is really a succession of rows. In Sinkers Row ... each house has three rooms, one large kitchen with cement floor, with two comfortable rooms upstairs in addition to a decent pantry. The houses in this part of Albion Row are also provided with backyards, ash-pits and privies much as they are met with in towns. They are the only houses in the village which are so provided. ... The other parts of Albion Row are not so creditable. ... You divide one house by partition and straight away, contrary to all rules of arithmetic, one house which was barely large enough for one family becomes two. The houses at Shankhouse are pretty liberally supplied with gardens ... 30 yards long, the width of the house at the front and 60 yards at the rear. Higher up the road is also a Primitive Chapel.* [93] *Behind Albion Row and Railway Row is Middle Row. ... inside, these wooden houses look roomy ... but the walls are so thin that they are easily penetrated by summer heat and winter cold ... a narrow ladder leads from the kitchen to the bedrooms. The village school is situated amid the old houses and in its present state is anything but a credit to the colliery. We are glad to observe, however, that the new school is rapidly approaching completion.'* [94]

---

[90] Mr. Ord's notes were transcribed by Mr. George Gate and provided by Mr. Ian Clough of North Heaton.

[91] Brannigan, *Ibid*, p.4.

[92] Image provided by Betty Norris.

[93] There were in fact three chapels in Shankhouse; Wesleyan, Primitive and United Methodist. The original place of Methodism was in a large house in Shankland Terrace. *Ibid*, Smith, p.25.

[94] Extract from *Newcastle Daily Chronicle*, 26th July 1873, p.2.

Continuing from the south end of Cramlington to Shankhouse any traveller on the Newcastle Road would find, on the east side, Colliery Farm and Shankhouse School. Further along there were a couple of houses, the post office and handy (hardware) shop. This last shop was on the very edge of Amelia Colliery's yard. Opposite the colliery were Shankhouse Club, Colliery Houses and the Chapel. At ninety degrees from these buildings were the wood rows of Shankhouse. These, and the other buildings on the west side of the road, were very close to the mineral railway line which led into the colliery. Beyond the colliery, proceeding north, on the east side of Newcastle Road were Jack Traise's barber shop and 2nd Cramlington Scout Hut.

Newcastle Road, Shankhouse. The un-metalled roadway leads towards the colliery.

Tucked beside the road, which is now classified A1061 and leads to Blyth, there was a tin, mission church which was linked with St. Nicholas Church in Cramlington Village and Mrs. Young's shop with the fish and chip shop run by Mrs. Brown near to the High Pit road. Dinah Patterson, 79 years, of Mayfield Terrace, writing in May 1985 recalled the tin church in verse:

> 'On Sundays we went to the little tin church
> St. Peter's by name. As we stood in the porch
> The smoke from the stove made us splutter and cough
> And really we felt it was not good enough,
> That our church could not be properly heated
> Without all this smoke with which we were greeted
> I suppose funds were low, it could not be afforded
> If only someone a gift had awarded
> To supply our church with central heating
> What a difference it would have made to our meeting.'

On the north side of the Blyth road was a further hardware shop and the Albion Inn, which was more commonly known as 'The Folly'. Bog Houses stood virtually in line with the wood rows on the east side of the Newcastle Road. Dinah Patterson listed some of the personalities of Shankhouse:

Shankhouse School teachers	Miss Polly Websell
	Miss Soppitt
	Miss Adeline Swann
	Miss Robertson
	Miss Reed
	Miss Sadie Endean
	Mr. Tommy Hedley (Head Teacher)
Clerk to Education Committee	Mr. Bill Robson
Primitive Chapel Minister	Mr. Kennedy
Doctor in Young's House, Hasting Terrace	Doctor Brown
Undertaker in Rose View	Mr. Alec Ferrow

And responding to a poem published in a local paper by Len Fletcher, Dinah wrote –

> 'I've just read your interesting rhyme,
> About old Shankhouse when in its prime.
> Where I played as a child in field and by burn
> And the school I attended – the object to learn.
> My headmaster then – Thomas Hedley by name
> (No taller than the pupils he tried hard to tame)
> Put fear into me when he picked up the stick
> For reading and writing and arithmetic.
> His copperplate writing was a joy to behold,
> I tried to copy it and often was told
> I did very well – my exercise book
> Frequently bore a remark on the pains that I took.' [95]

At the south end of the colliery village, if a traveller chose to turn east at Klondyke and go towards Seaton Delaval, he or she would pass the walled garden of Cramlington House (see page 21) on the left and the small, stone lodge which is now all that remains.

A couple of hundred yards further down the East Cramlington road, on the north side, would be found the school and the Methodist Chapel. Crossing the colliery line, next to the chapel, would lead to a further school on the south side and a Primitive Methodist Chapel. There were also 39 house in a straight line on the north side of the road and adjacent to it. Between the railway lines leading from the Ann Pit at Klondyke and the Amelia Pit at Shankhouse were 39 houses in Lamb Street. This street, named after the mine owner, was immediately adjacent to the main thoroughfare. Opposite, beside the Primitive Methodist Church and the Mechanics' Institute were Marjorie and Elizabeth Streets with 55 dwellings. On the other side of the rail network were Corving Row,[96] Office Row and Old Stone Road with a total of 54 houses. There was also a public house called Boundary Inn at the east end of Old Stone Road. Tucked away at the back of the colliery were Double Junction and Single Junction: further rows of 50 houses, more widely spaced and with larger gardens.

East Cramlington School.

---

[95] Dinah Patterson died 13th June 1989.

[96] A 'corve' was the basket or boggie into which coal was put for delivery out of the mine.

Dinah Newton Patterson in her poem written not long before she died, managed to cleverly encapsulate what life meant to her as a resident of a former mining village –

'A Picture of 'Canny' Shankhouse'

'At a heap of rubble I stand and stare
Remembering what had once stood there,
A humble home, in a longish street,
With gardens mostly bright and neat.
I hear young voices in the lane
Ropes are swinging once again
'Salt, cayenne, pepper' are the chanting calls,
As children skip and bounce their balls,
Two women are standing at the tap
While filling their pails they laugh and chat,
Then hurry up street with limping stride
Water spilling over either side.
I see the pit chimney so very high,
Silhouetted there against the sky.
Thick clouds of smoke drifting here then there,
As the breeze gently lifts it into the air.
The winding wheels hum as they spin around
Drawing the cage from underground.
Then they gradually slow and come to a stop,
And miners file out now they're at the top.
A buzzer blows and I can hear,
The clip clop of boots as the miners draw near.
Their faces are black, they look tired and worn,
But glad to see the light on this fine sunny morn.
A load of coal lies at each coalhouse door
Like little black hillocks right down to the store.
House chimneys are smoking, there's a good fire in the grate,
A pie in the oven and the bread has been laid.
The smell of dinner pervades the air
As the workers hurry to get their share,
Before off to bed for a well earned rest,
Satisfied that at least they had done their best.
I see sand-stoned steps all neat and clean
And streets swept up where the coal had been
Pit clothes being brushed and folded away
And boots scraped and greased ready for the next day
While standing here I remember all this,
The place of my childhood I sadly miss.
No more the old houses or gardens are seen
Just rubble and jungle where they have been.
I've an ache in my heart and a tear in my eye
As I leave happy memories of days gone by.'

RELIGION

Anglicanism

The Anglican Church, built in 1680 on the site of the former Norman Chapel, was described as being sufficient to *'accommodate all worshippers'*. It had *'glazed windows with shutters, slated nave, leaded chancel, rush covered floor and stone altar. There were candles for lighting and incense to sweeten the air.'* [97]

Old St. Nicholas Church.

Through time however, with the growth of the village the building was proving too small to accommodate the number of people who normally attended. In response to this, on 21st December 1843, Sir Matthew White Ridley, Bart,[98] chaired a meeting of principal landowners and residents in the village.

The meeting agreed that the population increases merited the building of a new church, sufficient to seat not less than 500 people. A public subscription was immediately commenced. By 1856 the necessary funds had been raised, and architect, Mr. John Dobson (right) of Newcastle was commissioned to draw plans for the church. He predicted that a new building would cost £2,600.

---

[97] Watson, *Ibid*, p.13.

[98] Sir Matthew White Ridley (whose image is shown earlier) was MP for Northumberland. He was a skilled farmer and he built many model farms including Milkhope and Horton Grange; also on his land were several coal mines. Despite his many responsibilities he generously gave of his time and expertise to local people and to good causes in his community.

The Church Building Society offered £170 and the owners of East and West Cramlington Collieries agreed to forward further subscriptions. The faculty for taking down the old building and constructing the new was granted by diocesan authorities on 25th July, 1865. Once the ground was cleared, Sir Matthew White Ridley, Bart., laid the foundation stone on 11th September, 1865. This was in the presence of Edward Potter, Hugh Taylor of Cramlington Hall and Shum Storey of Arcot House.

The architects were Austin and Johnson of Newcastle and the builders were Messrs Waterson and Stafford of Morpeth. Over the next three years the church was built. Whilst the church was being constructed, the tin mission church of St. Peter, at Shankhouse, was used.

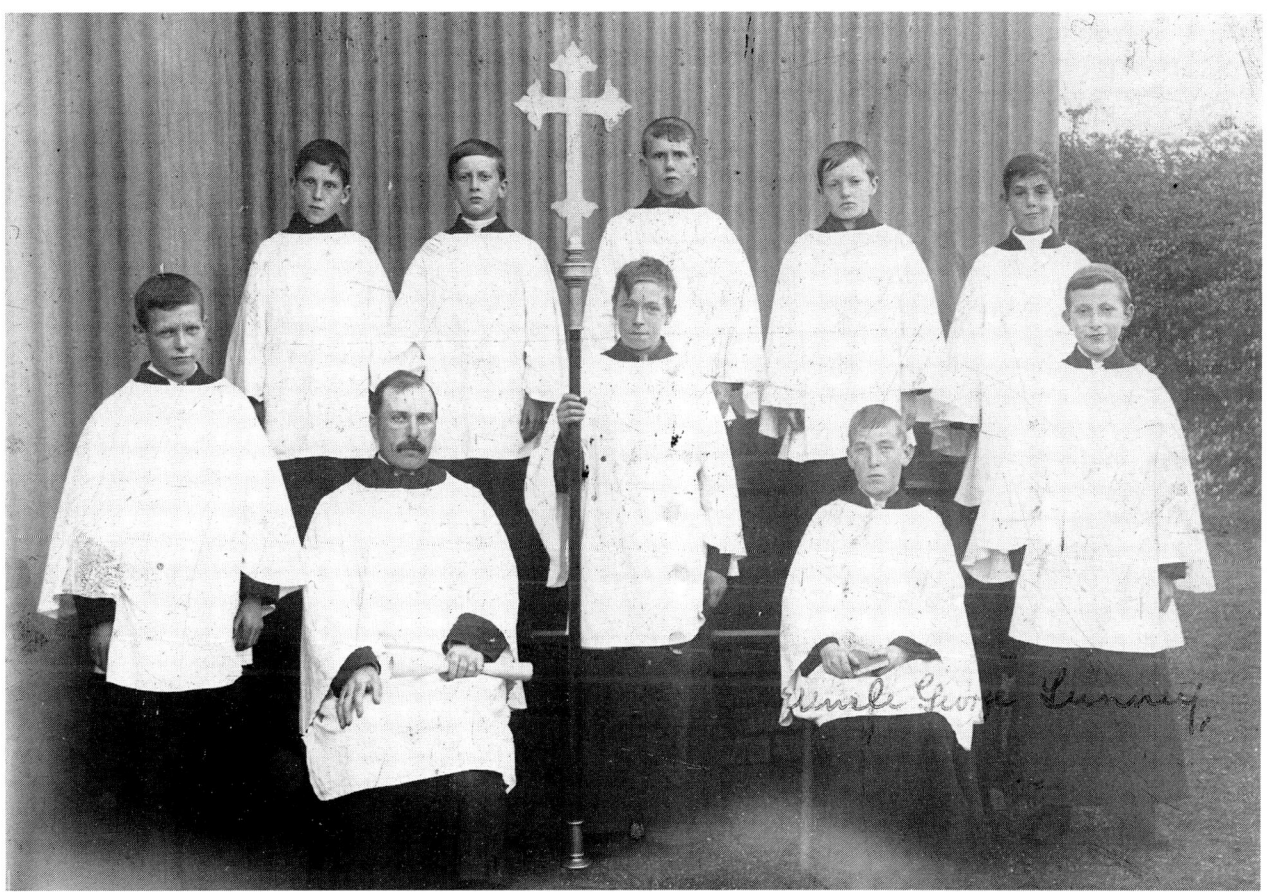

St. Peter's Choir outside the 'tin church'. George Tunney is seated on the right. [99]

Harriet[100] of Lookout Farm, Seaton Sluice, watched from afar whilst St. Nicholas Church was being built and wrote to her sister Eleanor in Durham on 17th May, 1868 telling her of her visit to the church to witness its consecration.

'From my bedroom window I have watched the tower being built … and my husband has teased me for being so interested. 'When the building is finished', he said, 'you must go to the first service'. … it was a lovely morning,[101] *birds singing, the hedgerows after the rain, washed dry. A fox crossed the road before us … the roadside was bright with wild flowers and patches of yellow broom. On our left side was the Tile Works, the Old Stone Row next, Office and Corving Row – past the Engine Pit and on to Lamb Street. Near the colliery wagon-way the Primitive Chapel and over the Wesleyan Chapel and the school – these two in one building. At Cramlington House (home of the Colliery Viewer) gardeners were setting plants. Here we turned towards Ann Pit with its few dwellings. Now before us I could see the new church from toes to top. I learned that the children had holiday for the special occasion. Seated almost in the centre I was able to*

---

[99] Image provided by Betty Norris.
[100] Harriet was Mr. Alf Smith's grandmother.
[101] St. Nicholas Church was consecrated on 12th May 1868.

see and hear the ceremony and service. The Lord Bishop[101] *was received at the main door by the Incumbent Rev. Smithard-Hind and other clergymen. A petition was presented by patrons of the church and churchwardens,*[102] *requesting that the bishop would consecrate the church and burial ground. The Bishop with the Diocesan Registrar, the incumbent and more than a dozen other clergymen proceeded to the Communion table. The Instruments of Conveyance, Donation and Endowment were received and placed on the Holy Table. My Lord Bishop then addressed the congregation. The bishop preached an excellent sermon; his text Hebrews 4:16.*[103] *Doctor Leggett of Newcastle played the harmonium and the choir of St. Mary's, Blyth assisted the local singers. At the close of the service the Lord Bishop proceeded to consecrate the church. After this the procession of clergy and lay officers reformed and walked to the burial ground and this also was consecrated. The church tower is 72 feet high; no wonder it can be seen from Seaton Sluice. The Blue Bell Inn and the Fox and Hounds had been lime washed (these were busy serving refreshments to visitors). The single storey stone cottages were quite gay in appearance – doors and shutters newly painted in a variety of colours. Flowering plants were displayed and even window sills had bonny stones and bits of crystal on show; all this decoration was said to be by order, to impress the bishop and other important visitors.'* [104]

St. Nicholas Church and graveyard in the Victorian period.

The family grave for Henry Shum Storey, Emma, George Henry and Gertrude Isabella Shum Storey, is in St. Nicholas Churchyard. There is also a large marble angel inside the church dedicated to the 'beloved memory of George Shum Storey who died in Malta on 18th December 1869, aged 28. The Potter grave is also in the churchyard of St. Nicholas.

In 1873 a clock and peal of six bells were installed in the tower in memory of Edward Potter of Cramlington House. The cost was borne by the workmen at Cramlington Collieries who agreed to a reduction of 2 shillings and 6 pence being deducted from their wages.

---

[101] Charles Thomas Baring was Bishop of Durham between 1861 and 1879. His father was one of the founders of Barings Bank. Bishop Baring was a fervent Evangelical who refused to licence curates to clergy whose ritual was contrary to his own interpretation of the Book of Common Prayer. He suspended the Rural Dean of Morpeth for wearing a stole of which he disapproved. Bishop Baring lived a life of devout simplicity and his episcopate was marked by his establishment of 102 new parishes and the building of 119 churches – including St. Nicholas at Cramlington.

[102] The church wardens were Edward Potter, Charles Carr, William Aubone Potter, John Wardle, William Hornsby and Robert Craig.

[103] Hebrews 4:16 'Let us therefore come boldly unto the throne of grace; that we may obtain mercy, and find grace to help in time of need.'

[104] Letter dated 17th May 1868 from Harriet of Seaton Sluice to her sister Eleanor in Durham – provided by Harriet's granddaughter.

Inside St. Nicholas' Church showing the rood screen with decorative carvings and stained glass behind. The carvings of Christ on the cross with Mary, his mother, and Mary Magdalene on either side, were added to the rood screen on 21st December 1895. The cost of £120 was met by Mrs. Aubone Potter. The stained glass windows are especially attractive having been made by Henry Mark Barnett of York; Daniel Cottier of Glasgow,[105] and Clayton Bell of London. The windows were paid for by land and mine owner families.

The funeral hatchment[111] shown on the right is for Adam Mansfeldt de Cardonnel-Lawson, who died in June 1820 aged 73 years and was buried at Cramlington on the 14th day of that month.[106] Originally the hatchment would have been displayed in the front of his home at Cramlington Hall and after the funeral, hung in the church. Black on the left side of the hatchment signifies that the man had died; white on the right shows that his wife, née Mary Kid was still living; and the closed helmet shows that Adam was a gentleman and not a knight or a peer.

---

[105] Nichol, Basil H., *A Guide to the Stained Glass Windows at St Nicholas Church Cramlington* (Cramlington, St Nicholas Church, 2000). A Cottier stained glass window is in Harvard Memorial Hall, America; a prestigious building built to commemorate Harvard men who fell in the Civil War.

[106] The hatchment must have been brought from the old St. Nicholas Church. When it was found in 1974 it was restored by students from Gateshead Technical College and hung in the present St. Nicholas Church.

Methodism

Old maps show the level of Christian commitment in Cramlington, with non-conformist chapels of two or more persuasions in each of the small colliery areas. Shankhouse, for example had Wesleyan, Primitive and United Methodist Chapels.

The beginning of Methodism in Cramlington is closely related to the beginning of the Methodist movement. John Wesley visited the district at Easter 1743 (five years after the founding of the movement) and preached to the miners of Plessey. He returned that July and on a number of subsequent occasions. In 1791, William Hunter a convert of Wesley, preached at Blyth, and in 1822 William Clowers, Evangelist of the newly formed Primitive Methodist Church came to the North East on an evangelistic mission.

The Primitive Methodist movement had its origins in Staffordshire, in 1811. It was characterised by zealous evangelism, spontaneous prayer and impromptu hymn singing, and it started as a reaction against the Wesleyan drive towards *'respectability and denominationalism'*. Primitive Methodism was a movement led by the poor for the poor. Adherents and followers were less likely to be controlled by central policy and Primitive Methodist preachers were mostly men (but sometimes children as young as fifteen) who emerged from congregations. They favoured plain dress and plain speaking as opposed to the Wesleyans' *'tendency for literary allusions and sermons delivered in high-flown language'*.[107]

'The building of the first Methodist Church at West Cramlington, and also the Primitive Methodist chapel (was in) 1851. After the site had been acquired from the colliery owners the men quarried the stones in their own time. On Saturdays they secured carts on hire or on loan and brought the stones to the site. Each night they placed sufficient stones on the scaffold for the masons to use the next day; the masons being supplied by the Colliery owners. The women, by working at sewing meetings holding teas etc, did their share in providing money for the various expenses needed in the project.

At Shankhouse a building in the middle of the High Row of Shankhouse Terrace had been set aside by the colliery owners in the early 1850s. This building was larger than the surrounding dwelling houses but on the building of the new Primitive Methodist Chapel near the colliery and school was converted into use. In 1858 there were three chapels recorded in Cramlington – at Cramlington Colliery, West Cramlington and Shankhouse.' [108]

The Lamb Colliery had a United Methodist Chapel, which was finalised in 1872, but had roots going back to 1859 when it was then linked to the school. Christians of the non-conformist, United Methodist persuasion had broken away from the Wesleyans in 1857 for constitutional rather than doctrinal reasons. Their style of worship amalgamated the practices of Wesleyan Association, Protestant Methodists and Wesleyan Reformers who had been expelled from the Wesleyans when charged with failing to follow the rigors of that church.

A Primitive Methodist Chapel in East Cramlington was built further east on the opposite side of the road in 1873. During the last 30 years of the 19th century Methodism continued to grow and the following chapels were built in Cramlington.

Cramlington Colliery United Methodists	1872
Caramlington Colliery Primitive Methodists	1873
West Cramlington Colliery United Methodists	
Shankhouse Primitive Methodists	
Shankhouse United Methodists	
Shankhouse Wesleyan Methodists	1870
Cramlington Village Wesleyan Methodists	1881
Cramlington Station Terrace Primitive Methodists	1893
Hartford Primitive Methodists	1903

---

[107] A summary of information drawn from Wikipedia and *The Concise Oxford Dictionary of the Christian Church* (Oxford, OUP, 1977), Ed. E.A. Livingstone, p.415.
[108] Laverick, J.G. (Cramlington, 1969) 'Souvenir Brochure of the Opening of Cramlington Methodist Church' on Saturday 6th December 1969, pp.6–7.

In Church Street in Cramlington Village was the Wesleyan Chapel. The principal foundation stone was laid by Lady Ridley on 17th October 1881. Supplementary foundation stones, in line with the base structure of the building, were laid by prominent people and engraved with their names, but 20th century footpaths have obscured some of them. Those which are visible include: Mrs. C. Morrison, Mrs. Jane Elstob, Mr. H. Patterson, Mrs. Mary Ann Willis and Mrs. Lizzie Lockwood.

Many leading men were lay-preachers and their faith had significant impact on their role in the community and in the workplace.

Alf Smith stated: '... *I can recall many remarkable men who entered public service and became leaders in local and county affairs and whose basic educational acquirement was obtained as a local preacher in the Methodist Circuit.*' [109]

110

[109] Smith, Alf., *Cramlington Through the Ages*, (Wooler, Glen Graphics, 2009), p.25.
[110] The 4th Baronet Ridley died in 1877. His wife Cecilia (née Parke) predeceased him by 32 years and he did not remarry. The above image (provided by Mr. Bob Downer, Blagdon Estates, and reproduced with permission) is of Mary Georgiana Ridley (née Majoribanks), who by then had become Lady Ridley, wife of 1st Viscount Matthew White Ridley (1842–1904). Viscount Ridley was Home Secretary between 1895 and 1900 when he was elevated to the House of Lords.

The Primitive Methodist Sunday School Hymn Book published in 1879 had in mind self-improvement as well as worship. The Preface states: *'It is earnestly hoped that the hymns thus brought together may prove a fitting medium whereby to express to God the soul's deepest and truest feelings; that as they are sung in our Schools, they may be attended with blessings; and when stored in the memory of our young people, they may remain with them to inspire and enrich their future life.'*

'1907 marked the centenary of Primitive Methodism and a camp was held at Seghill on Sunday 7th July. 3000 people assembled for the full day. The old hymns were sung. A love feast was held, prayer rings were formed and glory came down.' [111]

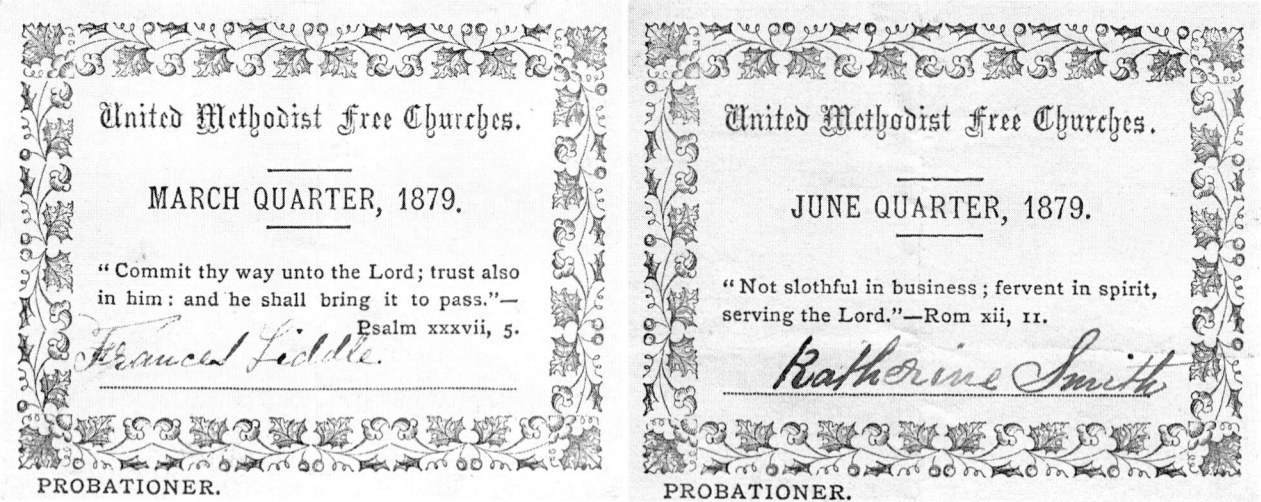

The United Methodist Free Churches had their own way of encouraging commitment. They did this through the quarterly issue of attendance tokens for the youngster who went to chapel.

Catholicism

By 1828 there were sufficient Catholics in the Seghill, Burradon, Dudley and Cramlington areas to cause Dominican Father Weldon to travel by horse and trap from Newcastle to say Mass at the old Blake Arms at Seghill. The arrival of Irish Catholic labourers, looking for work in the pits, further increased the number of regular churchgoers and this brought the first resident priest, Father O'Dwyer, to the area in 1858. In 1868, with the help of the Lamb mine owning family, who were prominent Catholics, a brick chapel and school were erected in Annitsford village.

In 1900, when Father Scott came to the parish he inherited a debt of £473. Mrs. Emmaline Shawe-Storey, (who had converted to Roman Catholicism) called to see Father Scott after attending Mass at the chapel school in Annitsford. She asked him how much the church was in debt, paid off what was owed, additionally gave him a cheque for £7,000 [112] and told him: *'To take the field on the north side of the reservoir, some half mile north of the village, and build a church where people can pray in peace.'*

Soon afterwards Father Scott was sent to Rome and the task of building the church fell to Father John H. Chapman. He and architect Mr. Parxous went to Ostend and came back with a design based on the cathedral there. They took the precaution of laying a concrete raft over what was known to be the previously mined ground and commenced building. The contractor was Mr. J. Ferguson of Newcastle.

---

[111] Laverick, *Ibid*, p.8.

[112] In 1900 £473 would be worth £349,273.64p and £7,000 would be worth £729,208.20p in 2013.

Father David Scott at the old Presbytery and School Chapel, *c.*1900.

The Foundation Stone of the church being laid by Bishop Collins.[113]

---

[113] The images of Father Scott, the laying of the foundation Stone and those inside the church were provided by Father Richard Harriot and are reproduced with permission.

The church was consecrated on 22nd June 1906. The *Newcastle Evening Chronicle* for Monday 25th June, 1906 reported: *'The service on Sunday was largely attended, amongst those present being Mrs. Shawe-Storey, the donor of the church who motored from Newcastle. Pontifical High Mass was celebrated, the Auxiliary-Bishop of Hexham and Newcastle (the Right Reverend Dr. Collins) being assisted by the Deacon and Sub-Deacon (the Rev. Father Mann and Dr. Burdess). After the celebration, in which the congregation joined, a sermon was preached by the rev. Father Maturin, of London, who based his discourse on verse 2, Chap.2 of Isaiah.* [114] *The Rt Rev. Dr Collins was the preacher at the afternoon service.'* [115]

St. John the Baptist, Annitsford.

St. John the Baptist's church is sometime referred to as the *'church among the trees'* because Mrs. Shawe-Storey instructed her gardeners to plant hedges and conifers in the grounds. Prior to her conversion to Catholicism, Emmaline Shawe Storey had been regular in her attendance at St. Nicholas Church in Cramlington Village and a generous benefactor there too.

Lady Chapel.

Altar St. John the Baptist Church.

---

[114] Isaiah 2:2 'And it shall come to pass in the last ddays, that the mountain of the Lord's house shall be established in the top of the mountain, and shall be exalted above the hills; and all nations shall flow into it.'

[115] Additional information drawn from Gatherer, Michael, *A Guide to the Church of St. John the Baptist – Throughout the Years*, (Cramlington, St. John the Baptist, 1996).

In the church baptistry is a memorial plaque to members of the Lamb family and nearby a plaque commemorating the deaths of Robert Ormston Lamb of Hayton House, Carlisle on 26th December, 1912, and his son Gerrard Joseph Lamb of the same address who was killed in action on December 1st 1914. Two of the stained glass windows above the altar are dedicated to members of the Lamb family; Robert Ormston Lamb, 1836–1912, and Richard Westbrook Lamb, 1826–1895.

Within the grounds of the church, is the cemetery which was in use before the church was built. Among the graves is that of Annitsford's internationally famous bass singer, Owen Brannigan.

INDUSTRIAL ACTION

Many of the mine owners and the colliery managers, professed Christian faith. They advocated truth and justice, love and social inclusiveness. But it was clear that they also believed in the ethic of hard work as a way towards self improvement. Work in the pits was hard; hours were long, uncomfortable and arduous. There were inequalities in pay, uncertainty in employment and poor housing. Inequalities, perceived injustices and inability to resolve disputes through negotiation, were regular sources of conflict for the miners which resulted in strike action. Richard Fynes expressed the plight of the miners:

> 'Stand firm to your union,
> Brave sons of the mine,
> And we'll conquer the tyrants
> Of Tees, Wear and Tyne
>
> We'll never leave the union field
> Until we make oppression yield.' [116]

In an historical survey carried out in 1963 by Mr. H.A. Taylor, Archivist for Northumberland County Council, it was recorded that between 1839 and 1865 – '... *the West Cramlington pit had had the best labour relations in the district (this was) despite the fact that they had been on strike 23 times. ... At this colliery, management was benign ... and the pitmen organised their day as they pleased and worked as long as they liked. However, in June 1865 industrial relations took a significant turn. The miners of Cramlington Colliery made application for an advance of one penny (and in some cases two pence) per ton of coal 'won' at the coal face. This was to put them on equal footing with colliers of other districts. When the coal owners refused this demand, once again the men went on strike.*' [117]

---

[116] Fynes, Richard, *The Miners of Northumberland and Durham*, (Sunderland, Thomas Summerbell, 1873), p.100.
[117] H.A. Taylor, *Cramlington – Historical Survey* (Newcastle, County Hall, 1963), p.4.

Thomas Hancock in 1983, reflecting on how families coped during strikes, wrote: *'During these periods without pay the routine was to eat sparsely. First you 'lived on your fat'. ... Then you used up the bit of money saved up in the Co-op share book. Next, the Co-op would extend credit ... to the value of dividend expected for a few years.'* [118]

Patrick Brannigan added: *'During the strike a 'bonanza' of heating material was discovered, An early coal washery had been installed at a nearby colliery, and in their washing process they had been able to clean and grade the coal, all except the fine pieces plus the dust. ... this material drained of water and the solids settled. Thus it was possible to mould it in the hands and bring it home to dry. ... it was known as 'Duff'. 'Duff' being the dialect word for dough as in 'plum dough'.'* [119]

As the strike proceeded, the mine owners looked for alternative means of creating a workforce. They sent representatives to Cornwall to recruit tin miners with a promise of increased wages, free housing, free coal and some household items. In the interim period further efforts were made to seek a compromise. However, when the pits remained idle for nearly sixteen weeks, notices were served on the men, informing them that they would have to vacate their houses within a given time. Though many had been expecting this, the notices caused considerable alarm. This stimulated new efforts to bring about reconciliation. The masters offered a second examination of the colliery by the arbitrators, on condition that the men agreed to recommence work pending independent investigation. This question was put to a large gathering of men at a meeting at the Astley Arms, Seaton Delaval on Tuesday 10th October 1865. After due consideration, a further meeting, with a larger contingency of workers, was called for the next morning. The mine owners' proposal was rejected by these men, who decided to hold out for their initial demands.

'Almost immediately the mine owners sent in bailiffs who were ordered to clear the mine workers' homes. The morning was wet and the roads black and boggy. When the bailiffs reached the home of Tommy Baulks, Treasurer of the Union, the pitmen crowding around, became understandably hostile and a general onslaught began. The men were aggravated to a very great extent by the insolence of the evicting party, who not content with entering the houses ... misbehaved themselves in a hundred different ways ... such as drinking milk and eating food which they found in some of the cottages, and on one occasion emptying some dirty slops out of a jug onto a mother and her children. A number of police were mounted and some of the women brought out their fire-blazers, and using pokers for banging, created a perfect panic. The terrified horses ... plunged and kicked, the pitmen shouted and yelled ... hooting and kicking the 'candymen' (bailiffs) and police. Stones fell as thick as hail ... and the evictions were suspended. On Tuesday 17th October a detachment of the 64th Regiment of the North Staffs Regiment arrived from Manchester to assist the police keep order at Cramlington. (And later, following arrests made during the initial skirmishes) six miners appeared at Newcastle Spring Assizes charged with causing a riot.

D. Moore was sentenced to nine months imprisonment.
T. Wandless and M.M. Glen each got eight months.
Alex Barrass, T. Dodds and T. Pringle each got six months.

Four other miners had their cases dealt with in the Magistrates Court at Alnwick, and on the Friday after the men had been brought before the Justices, the bailiffs, military and police recommenced the evictions. [120] *'The conduct of the men imprisoned in Morpeth Gaol greatly impressed the Governor and won his admiration. The Miner's Union paid out £4,290 in strike pay and levied 1s 6d a fortnight from its members to cover this. Membership was in fact stimulated by the need for funds and the union's previous membership of 4,000, in 20 collieries, rose to 16,000 during the strike.'* [121]

The first group of 300 Cornishmen with their families arrived in Cramlington on 5th December 1865 and a further batch of 128 men with their families of 111 women and 248 children came twelve days later.

---

[118] Hancock, *Ibid*, p.21.
[119] Brannigan, *Ibid*, p.18.
[120] Fynes, Richard, *The Miners of Northumberland and Durham – A history of their social and political progress*, (Wakefield, S. R. Publishing, 1873), pp.248–253.
[121] Unpublished history and memoir of *'The Hancock Family of Cramlington'*, by Thomas Hancock, dated 1st November 1983, p.2. Hancock, *Ibid*, p.23 (drawn as a secondary source from Fyne).

Local miners who could not find accommodation with families initially planned an encampment in nearby fields but local publicans came forward and offered the men and their families all their spare rooms. In this manner, most of the men, women and children were housed in comparative comfort. The Cornish families were not equally comfortable, indeed they were instantly unpopular. Not only were they taking the jobs and homes of local people –

'the men didn't wear traditional pit clothes and had to be taught how to work the pit …'

'Cornish women's attempts at making bread were mocked (but it had to be admitted that they were 'tops' at making pasties.)'

'The foreigners were not welcome in the pubs, Chapels or even Co-op store and it took years for them to be accepted, but they had to stay because there was no work for them in the West Country.' [122]

Initially the Cornish families were housed in Terrace Row, which through time became known among locals as Cornish Terrace.

Slowly, over an extended period, largely due to friendships forged by children in the disparate communities, relationships improved and the Cornish folk became more accepted.

Incoming miners (and local ones when the industrial disputes were settled) endured the same conditions of employment underground. And during these times, life in the colliery villages often followed identifiable routines with the hours marked by the sounds and smells associated with the 'winning' of coal.

'Buzzers called the surface workers to and from work and announced their bait times. … Different pits blew their buzzers at a stipulated time; Seghill at 7.30p.m., High Pit at 8 p.m., Wrightson at 9 p.m. [123]

Not every one had clock, so a 'knocker up' used to go around the streets during the night to ensure that workers got a call. Some districts had a slate built into the wall at the back door so that the occupier could chalk up the time required to call.' [124]

THE CO-OPERATIVE SOCIETY [125]

Miners' wages were low, the price of provisions was high and goods were often available through outlets controlled by the mine owners – and miners' homes were poor. This promted the miners to turn their thoughts towards founding a Co-operative Store. Their reading of a little book entitled *'Self Help'* – and another called *'The History of Co-operation in Rochdale'*, roused them into action. They had many questions: how could a store be carried on successfully in a colliery district where employment was so precarious; how could inexperienced men hope to cope with the intricacies of business, and above all where were the funds going to come from? But they pressed on and on 5th January 1861, in the Blue Bell Inn, West Cramlington, they held a public meeting. Here it was agreed that a Co-operative Store *'be established at once'*.

The men took subscriptions of five shillings and six pence and when they had amassed £23 it was decided to open their first shop. At first they exercised a degree of caution, renting their first premises from Richard Fynes, who had done much in proposing and supporting the creation of the Co-op. After taking possession of his premises they spent £7 in providing fixtures.

---

[122] *Cramlington Yesterday Society Newsletter* number 38, August 2000 – using material drawn from the writing of Peter Dodds and Thomas Hancock.
[123] The evening buzzers indicated that the workmen at that particular colliery were not required for the next shift.
[124] Hancock, *Ibid*, p.24.
[125] The images of the Co-op reproduced here are from Mr. Alan Lowther's collection or from W. Simpson's *Short History of the Cramlington District Co-operative Society Limited, Jubilee Souvenir – 1861–1911*, (Manchester, CWS, 1912) provided by Malcolm and Daphne Morrison.

Many other meetings were held and ultimately a provisional committee was appointed to oversee the commencement of 'The Store':

John Bennett	Chairman
Joe Bell	Secretary
Bill Nicholson	Treasurer
J. Richardson	Committee
T. Armstrong	Committee
W. Urwin	Committee
J. Auld	Committee
M. Lowther	Committee
W. Rutherford	Trustee
C.H. Gregory	Trustee
J. Johnson	Trustee

On 21st March 1861, two members, in a cart which had been loaned by farmer Bell, set off for Newcastle to buy groceries and provisions. Within hours of their return, the produce had been snapped up by the miners' wives and within three months the pioneers had trebled their orders and had 66 members. On October 14th 1861, Mr. Crisp was appointed manager and a further two rooms were rented from Richard Fynes. In January 1862 it was decided to purchase the whole of Mr. Fynes' property, and two months later the building was bought for the sum of £60. By then the membership had increased to 80 and the manager had an assistant and a boy giving help in the store.

Early pioneers of Cramlington Co-operative.

The first Co-op, opened 1861.

Towards the end of 1863 the butchering business of the Co-op was being run from the Fox and Hounds Inn; and drapery business was being conducted from two adjoining houses which the Society had acquired.

The first drapery and tailoring shop.[126]

Annitsford Butchers.

---

[126] The first premises were in Smithy Square in the building occupied in 2013 by Renown Estate Agent.

Before too long, branches of the Cramlington Cooperative were opened in each of the districts of the town.

Shankhouse premises, *c*.1912.

Cramlington Colliery Branch.

The above plan[128] of the western section of Cramlington Village shows where the various Co-operative buildings were prior to the development of the town in the 1960s. Opposite where the Traveller's Rest public house is situated (now renamed John the Clerk) the whole complex of buildings were owned by the Co-operative Wholesale Society, including the garage in the bottom left hand section of the drawing. In the upper right section of the drawing, beyond Phillipson's Garage were the Co-op barns and stables.

Stables and workshops which included the blacksmiths' joiners' and paint shops.

---

[127] Map copied from Alan Lowther's collection. Much of the land previously occupied by the Co-op is now converted to car parks for Manor Walks shopping centre.
[128] Unfortunately the drawing still has someone's arithmetic visible on the top!

The Co-op installed a Gas Works Plant for their own use and in 1893 the plant was enlarged and gas mains were laid throughout the whole village.

Cramlington Village Square.

MANAGERESSES.

MANAGERS OF SOCIETY.

Houses owned by the Co-operative Society.

Cramlington Colliery Cottages.

East View Avenue.

Co-op delivery vehicles outside the Co-op garage.

Workmen painting one of the Co-operative Society's horse-drawn vans. They are being helped by soldiers who were stationed in Cramlington during the First World War and believed to be from the West Yorkshire Regiment.

Pictured during the 1926 strike, one of the motor delivery trucks (complete with starting handle and solid tyres) used by the Cramlington Co-op. The men are Stan Webster and Michael Neary.

The first van bought by the Co-op.

Jack Morrison, driver with Cramlington Co-op.[129]

The Greengrocery cart at Cramlington Gala.

---

[129] Photograph supplied by Malcolm and Daphne Morrison.

George Anderson (the flower man) at Cramlington Gala.

Shankhouse Co-op delivery horse and trap, with the colliery in the background.

TRANSPORT

Numbered A114 in the United Automobile Services fleet, AH 0673 was an AEC Y-type with a 32-seat Dodson body new around 1920. It was one of many built up from First World War chassis, surplus to military requirements after 1918. Unusually for a United bus, it appeared to have a quiet life, the body being sold at the end of 1927 and the chassis disposed of a month or so later for rebodying by its new owner, as a lorry.

PW 104 had an interesting history. It was numbered C72 in the United fleet and was an ex-War Department Daimler CB model, fitted with a 26-seat bus body built by United in 1923. It would have been fitted with pneumatic tyres before entering service as a bus or soon after, as new Daimler buses were being supplied on pneumatics by 1924. After it was withdrawn in 1929, the chassis was sold to Thomas & Evans (Corona lemonade) of Porth in South Wales, presumably for use as a lorry. Although it was licenced in September 1934, it reappeared in preservation in the 1960s/70s as a lorry with Watts of Lydney (the family which had owned the large Red & White bus company operating in South Wales, Gloucestershire and elsewhere from the 1920s to 1950).

Charles Moat with one of the pit ponies at East Cramlington.[130] The pit pony was from the 'horse hospital' between the High Pit and East Cramlington Farm.

Doctor Forsyth was employed by Cramlington Coal Company and treated patients in Cramlington and the surrounding villages, travelling by horse and trap. The colliers paid for the doctor's services.

Doctor Forsyth doing his rounds.[131]

William Muckle writing in 1981 said: *'I don't know how much it is now, but every man paid a shilling (to the union) and he also paid a shilling towards the doctor.'* [132] Dr Forsyth was a bachelor. His housekeeper was Miss Kitty Carter, a local woman. She also helped in his surgery. For the whole of Cramlington, he was surgeon, dentist, anaesthetist, midwife; and it was common whilst doing his rounds for him to call at a farm to buy eggs and vegetables to take to a needy patient. In his surgery he would often dole out to the children an apple or a banana to keep them occupied. He kept a parrot which spoke with the same Scottish accent and poor Miss Carter made many unnecessary returns to his surgery, unsure whether it was the Doctor or the parrot calling for 'Kitty'.' [133]

He died in 1927. His tombstone in Cramlington Churchyard bears the words 'Beloved practitioner of this parish.'

---

[130] Image from Laura Hancock's collection.

[131] The small boy to the right of the horse is George Stephenson who became the reporter who wrote some of the articles recorded in this book.

[132] Muckle, Ibid, p.19.

[133] Extracted from an undated copy of a George Stephenson article in the *Blyth News* and *Ashington Post* from the files of Cramlington Yesterday Society.

Writing for Cramlington Yesterday Society in 1998 Albert Foster stated: '*At Shankhouse in the 1920s the Doctor's surgery was in the back room of Mrs. Young's house. The yard was the waiting room, but if it was raining and Mrs. Young felt generous, she let patients into her wash house. Mr. Jim Ferrow, the Undertaker bought a Standard Ten car, the back window of which opened. When there was a stretcher case for the hospital in Newcastle, the recumbent patient was pushed through the opened window, with his or her nose very close to the roof. This same vehicle served as a hearse. Doctors carried out many minor operations on the kitchen table. My brother was born with rickets and mother was told to take him to the seaside to splash water on his legs. Pepper was used, blown down a patient's throat to ease tonsillitis; and poultices made of bread, mustard seed, linseed oil and kaolin, applied scalding hot were used to draw out skin infections. Outbreaks of measles, chickenpox, diphtheria and whooping cough were common, and scarlet fever and mumps. These went through the place like a plague and many had to spend weeks in isolation hospitals.*'

Ella Potts, reporting at the same time, said: '*Scarlet fever was a nasty illness … huge pieces of skin would peel off my feet. My parents had to stand outside the hospital and wave through the window. When there was an epidemic you went to see Doctor Quinn in Blagdon Terrace. You asked the bus driver to drop you off at Doctor's Corner.*'

Gwen Barrass records: '*T.B. was rife and many families had one member living in isolation in a shed at the bottom of their garden. If you had a red blanket on you and you were taken to hospital in an ambulance, it was presumed by onlookers that you had diphtheria.*'

The Hearse.[134]

---

[134] The Cramlington Coal Company kept its own hearse and horses for use amongst the villages. It was commonly kept in a building in High Pit Row.

RAIL TRAVEL

The start of rail travel is generally acknowledged as the opening of the Stockton to Darlington line in 1825. This was followed by lines connecting Liverpool and Manchester in 1830. By 1845 there were 2,441 miles of rail track laid providing new opportunities for trade and travel. Cramlington benefited from the laying of the Berwick to Newcastle line. Cramlington Station was opened on 1st July 1847, the first station master being Joseph Mundy.

The Flying Scotsman passing through Cramlington in the 1960s.

Cramlington Station, *c.*1940.[135]

---

[135] Images from Susan Napier's collection.

Entrance to the station yard. The houses on the right are Station Terrace.

The gable end of the large building on the left is of the old Railway Tavern. In the foreground is the goods shed, ticket office and rest room close by. The houses on the right were demolished soon after this photograph was taken c.1957.

136 Images from Susan Napier's collection.

Station Road led from the village to the station and parallel with the road was Station Terrace. Access to the main entrances to the properties was via an arch. Nelson Pit heap is in the background.

Back Station Terrace. The upper stories of the properties in Station Terrace were accessed via a steep and slippery ladder.[137]

Station Terrace from the west.

---

[137] Images from Susan Napier's collection.

SCHOOLS AND EDUCATION

The Church of England National Society, which had been formed in 1811 for the purpose of aiding education, helped St. Nicholas Church to open the first school in Cramlington. Two classrooms were provided in the building adjoining the church. The schoolmaster was Mr. Waddle.

In 1853 Mrs. Shum Storey of Arcot Hall opened the Cramlington National School for Girls and provided a teacher's house and an endowment of £30 a year. The headmistress was Miss Margaret McKenzie. Her house was built on the east side of the school. Eventually the school buildings were taken over by Cramlington Coal Company and then in 1902 by the County Council.

In 1849 Humble Lamb built a small day school for colliery children at West Cramlington, enlarged in 1855 to accommodate more children and again in 1873. That same year a school was built at Shankhouse. Later one was built at Hartford Colliery.

During 1885 Cramlington Coal company spent £1,142 on alterations to their schools to provide accommodation for 1,288 school children. Fees for the children's education were charged at between fourpence and eightpence a week, with the Guardians of the schools paying for the poor children. When the pits were idle, the fees were reduced to a penny a week. These fees were abolished once the government undertook responsibility for education and schools.

Children and teachers from West Cramlington School, *c*.1900.

West Cramlington School.

Shankhouse School, class II – George Tunney 3rd from left in the back row, *c.*1910.[138]

---

[138] Image from Betty Norris's collection.

Shankhouse School, *c.*1915 – Dinah Pattison (née Newton) 2nd left in the front row.

Shankhouse School 1917-18. John George and Isabella Dixon 2nd and 3rd from the right in the second front row.[139]

---

[139] Image from Laura Hancock's collection.

Education and self improvement was not just for children. Mechanics' Institutes were established in the mining communities to provide adult education, particularly in technical subjects, for working men. These were mostly funded by industrialists in the expectation that they would ultimately benefit from having a more knowledgeable and skilled workforce. The institutes contained vocational and inspirational reading matter and later popular fiction and non-fiction. These institutes were precursors to the public libraries which following the Public Libraries Act of 1850 provided public borrowing for women too. The institutes were also a venue for lecture courses and the display of museum pieces.

The Mechanics' Institute in Cramlington Village (above) was opened on 22nd December 1894 by Lady Ridley. There were Mechanics' Institutes in each of Cramlington's 'villages' and prior to the building of the Mechanics' Institute, Sir Matthew Ridley had given the men the use of rooms in Cramlington.

'The Institute (in the Village) had 30 members and their secretary was Mr. Edward Shotton. The Rev'd Smetherd, Incumbent of St. Nicholas Church, had been instrumental in helping the members and he and neighbouring gentry had presented the Institute with a number of standard books to serve as the nucleus of a library. (At) East Cramlington there is an excellent reading room ... the Secretary being Mr. William Hobkirk ... with eighty one members. The library which has only been in existence three years (although the reading room is much older) contains 236 good books. At West Cramlington ... there is a very excellent reading room, which number fifty one members, almost every young man about the colliery being in connection with it. Mr. Johnson acts as secretary, and the room is well supplied with newspapers. There are 230 volumes of good books in the library, and the manager of the colliery, Mr. Hurst, takes a lively interest in the progress of the institution.' [140]

During his membership of Cramlington Yesterday Society Alan Lowther interviewed 'Joe' who was born in Cramlington Village in 1901, the family later moving to 21 East Wood Row, next to the Lamb Pit in East Cramlington.

'When 'Joe' started school aged 6, it was at the little school, which later was the institute. Next it was the 'big' school, close to the Chapel. There were 90 pupils in his infant class at the little school and 'Ganny Forbes' the teacher there was so small she had to stand on a stool to write on the blackboard. At noon there was free broth provided. This was made from the meat bones donated by the local co-op butchers and vegetables given by the allotment holders. The broth was cooked on the premises in a great boiler. The road past the Lamb Street

---

[140] Extract from *The Daily Chronicle* and *Northern Counties Advertiser*, Wednesday 26th September 1860 – Our Colliery Villages Number II.

towards Seaton Delaval was known as the Green Lonnen. Just before the first right bend there was a hut where Mr. Parker sold fish and chips. Next to the Dolly Heap was a pond called 'the howdy-dowdy.' Youngsters used to bathe in it. In the middle was thick, yellow mud from the colliery waste heaps. Boys used to steal rides on the wagon sets running along the colliery line from Amelia pit and Joe Beattie, the Colliery Policeman's son fell off and the wagon ran over his arm and cut it off. He picked it up and ran home with it.' [141]

In 1902 work began on the building of the Council School (later known as Parkside School) which was behind the Blue Bell (Blagdon Inn). It opened in 1909 and provided education on the ground floor for juniors and on the upper floor for seniors. Each floor had its own headmaster. The children from the old schools at Cramlington and West Cramlington were transferred to here.

Council School showing soldiers billeted there during the First World War.

---

[141] There is no further mention of this poor boy's plight or progress (details extracted from the transcript of Alan Lowther's presentation to Cramlington Yesterday Society in 2002).

BRITAIN AT WAR

During the Great War of 1914–1918 the first airborne raid on Great Britain by the Germans occurred over Great Yarmouth in January 1915 when there were four fatalities. The second Zeppelin raid occurred over the North East coast.

'On April 14th 1915 Heinrich Mathy was in charge of the Zeppelin L9 airship. His mission was to bomb Tyneside's heavy industrial areas which were supporting the war effort. Members of the Northern Cyclist Battalion ... stationed at Cambois attempted a few shots but L9 continued over part of Blyth. It was seen so low over Horton that it could have been hit by a catapult, and continued over East Hartford. It headed up Scott Street (East Hartford) and then headed towards Cramlington Village. The first bomb was dropped in a field opposite Turnbull's Farm on Crawhall Lane, then others in Low Main Place and Bells Yard.' [142]

There was a second raid on Tuesday 15th June 1915 at 11.30pm.

On Friday 16th April 1915, *The Illustrated Chronicle* reported the Zeppelin attack.

'The German Zeppelin was first sighted around 7pm on Wednesday 14th April, three miles off the Tyne by the pilot of the cutter 'Protector'. It was steering a course N.N.W, apparently making for Blyth.'

The Chronicle's report continued –

'ZEPPELIN'S FLIGHT OF 800 MILES TO BOMBARD GRASSLAND!

The Zeppelin passed over Blyth where they dropped 8 bombs which fell harmlessly outside the town. ... It would be about 8.20pm when it arrived over Cramlington where, it is stated, no fewer than nine exploded bombs have since been collected. Mr. G Sims, who was attending choir practice in the Wesleyan Chapel heard the explosion, and rushing out with the rest, saw the Zeppelin over the chapel. It was, he said, a horrible thing to look at. One bomb dropped into a field on the West Farm, occupied by Mr. Hall, but did no damage beyond ploughing a hole in the ground. Within two minutes after the first explosion, another bomb was dropped. This fell into a field on the West Farm, occupied by Councillor Reid, and did more harm than the first. It struck a barn, penetrating the roof and set fire to the interior. Fortunately the fire was soon extinguished, though there was a danger that the consequences might have been serious, as two cottages abut the barn.

SHOTS AT THE AIRSHIP

The third bomb was thrown within a few minutes, the three being within the space of ten minutes. It fell harmlessly into a field in the neighbourhood of West Cramlington. The troops turned out and a number of shots were fired in the direction of the Zeppelin. Sergeant Marshall and the two special constables did everything possible in the way of darkening the village and making the air raid as futile as possible.'

In the course of that evening the Zeppelin visited other villages and towns nearby, including Choppington, Hartford, Dinnington, Benton, Wallsend and South Shields.

The article continued:

'There will, no doubt be great rejoicing in Germany, if the venturesome Zeppelin, which paid a fleeting visit to the North-East Coast on Wednesday, has returned in safety to the Fatherland.

The panic which it was hoped would result has not materialised. Nor was the damage caused in any way commensurate with the trouble the Germans must have taken.'

---

[142] Smith, *Ibid*, p.22.

Zeppelin damage at Bell's Yard, West Farm.

Sergeant Marshall with farm staff.

Bombs 18 inches by 9 inches diameter.

ZEPPELIN RAID, APRIL 14th, 1915.
Hole caused by bomb at Cramlington. Circumference 45 feet. Depth 5 feet (Z4)

---

[143] Second left is Tom Redhead.

Soldier at Stickley Farm.

Corporal Leach at Amelia Colliery, c.1915. He was billeted at Shankhouse Co-op buildings. Stan Webster is in the background.

---

144 Image from Betty Norris's collection.

The Great European conflict of the First World War saw a large number of miners from Cramlington volunteering for service. *The Iron and Coal Trades Review* newspaper for 30th July 1915 reported: *'Whole regiments had been recruited from colliery districts and there was one regiment in which every private was a pitman, every officer was connected with a colliery and the commanding officer himself was one of H.M. Inspectors of Mines. On the whole, miners have contributed 250,000 men to the new armies.'*

One hundred and seventy six soldiers from Cramlington did not survive the hostilities.

The war memorial bears 148 names and the plaque in St. Nicholas Church contains 62 names of which 34 are repeated from the external cenotaph.

The memorial was unveiled in 1922. Doctor Forsyth is among the local dignitaries and is seated in the forefront, wearing a top hat. The building on the right is the Blagdon Arms, and in the centre, in the background, is the original Wesleyan Chapel. The Parish Magazine for February 1921, written by the vicar on 19th January provides details of the memorial erected in memory of those who died.

'It is a very handsome Tablet, the general design workmanship of which has been beautifully and artistically executed. The material of the Tablet is white Sicilian marble fastened to a background of black marble. It contains in thee columns the names of sixty two former parishioners of Cramlington who fell in the Great war, many of whom were members of the Church. The Memorial was dedicated to the Glory of God and in memory of the fallen on Sunday January 16th by the Lord Bishop of Newcastle.

'… The total cost of the memorial is rather under £150 … and wish to add my sincere thanks to collectors and contributors to the fund, and to Messrs. Endean and Son, for their great courtesy and for the efficiency with which they have carried out the work.'

Memorial Plaque in St. Nicholas Church.

The Memorial in The Council (Parkside) School is in brass and oak, was made by Edward H. Thew Ltd of Dean Street, Newcastle and paid from contributions made by pupils at the school in memory of 'Old-boys' who lost their lives in the Great War.

At the end of the Great War communities celebrated in different ways. Cramlington erected several Victory Arches.

The Victory Arch, East Cramlington. The houses in Lamb Street on the left were demolished in 1955. The bridge in the foreground came down around 1960 and the Primitive Methodist Chapel seen on the right was taken down in 1955.

Victory celebrations in Paradise Row, 1919.[145]

Peace celebrations[146] – Rita Morrison (née Stephen) standing second from left.

---

[145] Image from Susan Napier's collection.

[146] Image provided by Malcolm and Daphne Morrison.

THE GENERAL STRIKE AND THE TRAIN DERAILMENT

On 30th June, 1925, on a national scale, the mine owners announced that they intended to reduce miners' wages.

'The coal owners gave notice of their intention to end the wage agreement then operating, bad though it was, and proposed further wage reductions; the abolition of the minimum wage principle, shorter hours and a reversion to district agreements from the then existing national agreements. This was without question, a monstrous package attack, and was seen as a further attempt to lower the position not only of miners but of all industrial workers.' [147]

The General Council of the Trade Union Congress responded by promising to support the miners in the dispute with their employers. The Prime Minister, Stanley Baldwin, stated that the subsidy to the miners' wages would only last nine months. In the meantime, the government set up a Royal Commission under Sir Herbert Samuel to look into the problems of the mining industry. The Commission reported in March 1926 and recommended the need for the mining industry to be re-organised. It rejected, however, the need for nationalisation. The Commission's report also recommended that the government subsidy should be withdrawn and the miners' wages reduced. Within the month, mine owners published new terms of employment, including an extension of the working day, district wage agreements and the reduction in the wages of all miners. These cuts were between 10% and 25%, depending on factors such as working conditions, difficulties in 'winning' coal and incidental benefits ancillary to pay. The mine owners announced that if the miners did not accept these new terms and conditions, then from the first day of May, they would be locked out of the pits.

William Muckle in his *'No Regrets'* records: *'Up here in Northumberland we were getting six shillings and nine and a half pence per shift and a 40% reduction in pay was on the cards from the mine owners. The pits were wet with foul air. There was no yearly or statutory holiday pay. There were no pit head baths. We lived in cramped houses and the toilets were earth closets and water was drawn from a standpipe 30 feet from the house. The balloon went up and we came out on strike. All lorries carrying coal were stopped and tipped. Sometimes the lorries were filled with police … but as time went on you always got some blacklegs.'* [148]

The Trade Union Congress met on 1st May 1926 and afterwards announced that a General Strike 'in defence of the miners' wages and hours' was to begin two days later. Sir Herbert Stanley approached the T.U.C. and offered to bring the strike to a close with a set of proposals, including: a National Wages Board with an independent chairman; a minimum wage for colliery workers; displaced miners to be given alternative employment; the wages subsidy to be re-instated whilst negotiations proceeded. On 11th May 1926, the T.U.C. accepted these proposals, but the miners did not.

'On May 10th, 1926 a meeting of the Cramlington Lodge was held in the Miners; Institute. One of the lodge officials ended the meeting with A.J. Cook's slogan, 'Stop the wheels turning'.' [149]

Nationally, the General Strike was called off, but the miners continued. However, by October 1926 hardship forced the miners to drift back to the mines. By the end of November most had reported back to work. However, many were victimised and remained unemployed for several years. Those that were re-employed were forced to accept longer hours, lower wages and district agreements.

Muckle's account continues: *'After, (the meeting) on the steps, I called for them all to come back after dinner and have a rail up to stop the blackleg coal trains going through. We returned about 1.30pm and just as we all met, we saw blackleg platelayers working in their 'plus fours' on the line. We stoned and chased them away. Then someone called out, 'Come on lads, we'll have a rail out.' Between twenty and thirty of us took the rail out. I and three others broke into the railwaymen's cabin and stole the gear in the morning (before the meeting) for the job in the afternoon. We took the rail up in record time, but we thought it was a coal train that was coming. We were amazed when it turned out to be the Flying Scotsman.'*

---

[147] Paynter, Will, 1925 – supporter of A.J. Cook, National Union of Mineworkers' general secretary.
[148] Muckle, William, *No Regrets*, (Newcastle, People's Publicaations, 1981) p.33.
[149] Muckle, *Ibid*, p.33.

The location of the derailment was one mile 632 north yards from Annitsford Station and 1,418 yards south of Cramlington Station; or 88 yards south of the railwaymen's cabin[150] referred to by Muckle as the place from which he stole the tools required for lifting the rail.

'The scab plate layers ran about 400 yards up the line, stopped the train and warned them there was something likely to happen … they stopped the train close to Cramlington Station. The train came on and we were standing behind a bush. It was derailed and when I looked around I was standing by myself. They (the passengers) were shouting out of the train, there were about 281 passengers I think on the train. When it started to sway, I was away! The engine went right up to the signal cabin … about one hundred yards further. I think the drivers jumped off. The engine flopped over and damaged the signal cabin. The buffers of the engine were in the earth.' [151]

The engine was the '*Merry Hampton*', a Pacific type, Number 2565 with an eight wheel tender and a combined weight of 148 tons 15 cwt. It was pulling twelve corridor coaches of the London and North Eastern Railway with a total weight of 522 tons 15 cwt.

After the derailment the engine lay on its left side, still coupled to the tender, but with the bogies ripped off. The first also lay on its side but still coupled to the tender. The second carriage also had its bogies ripped off and stood at right angles to the track. The third carriage stood upright with its front bogie wheels broken. The fourth coach was derailed across the down track.

[152]

---

[150] Details extracted from the London and North Eastern Railway's Inspector's report to the Ministry of Transport, 7 Whitehall Gardens, London, SW1, dated 27th May 1926.
[151] Muckle, *Ibid*, p.34
[152] Image from *Newcastle Evening Chronicle*, May 1926 – reproduced with permission.

153

154

155

153 Image from *Newcastle Evening Chronicle*, May 1926 – reproduced with permission.
154 Gatherer, Michael, *Ibid*, p.19.
155 Image from Susan Napier's collection.

The *Newcastle Evening Chronicle*'s article for Tuesday 11th May, 1926, carried the headline –

WHEN DESPAIR LED TO DESTRUCTION.

… The deliberate derailment with malice aforethought, of the pride and joy of the LNER – the passenger-laden Flying Scotsman. Men now alive in Cramlington came within an ace of committing the biggest mass murder in British history. They must look back on it now in the manner of men who have stood on the hangman's drop when it failed to function.'

The North Mail edition of the *Newcastle Daily Chronicle* for the same day provided the names of the driver and firemen as Bob Sheldon, Robert Aitken and Charles H. Hind. The only passenger to be hurt was Arthur Hamilton of 7, Whitehall Place, London. He had to be dug out from beneath the wreckage and had an injury to his leg which was stitched on the spot by a doctor. It took a few weeks of investigation (Muckle says five but this cannot be correct) before arrests were made.

'I remember that Saturday night. I left home about four o'clock to meet a girl at Cullercoats. Three lads were standing against a pub and one said, 'Have a good night for your last one. One of our mates had turned King's Evidence to save his own skin. He had a brother a policeman, and an uncle an Inspector of police.' [156]

John Hope Pool's hat displayed on the station master flag used on 10th May 1926.

Mr. Pool has endorsed the inside of the leather hat band as follows: *'I John Hope Pool wore this hat as assistant guard on the 10am Edinburgh to Kings Cross Express which was wilfully wrecked at Cramlington on May 10th 1926. I was in the employ of LNER during the General Strike acting as guard between York and Edinburgh on the Express.'*

---

[156] Muckle, *Ibid*, p.42.

Muckle was arrested at 1.30am on a Sunday morning and taken to Gosforth Police Station. Seven other men joined him there. They were later charged and remanded to Durham Prison.

On Thursday 2nd July 1926 the *Journal and North Star* newspaper reported the conclusion of proceedings at Newcastle Assize Court the previous day:

> *'TRAIN WRECKERS*
> *SENTENCED.*
> *Cramlington Miners Sent to*
> *Penal Servitude.*
> *WOMEN FAINT AND SOB*
> *Only Short of*
> *Murder.'*

Mr. Justice Wright, passing judgement on convictions based on conclusive evidence said: *'How young men like you, apparently well-behaved and respectable, could put into execution so nefarious a scheme has entirely been beyond my comprehension. I would be false to the charge committed to me if I dealt lightly with the crimes of which you have been found guilty.'*

The sentences were:

Name	Age	Sentence
Arthur Wilson	(27 years)	8 years penal servitude
Robert Harbottle	(21 years)	8 years penal servitude
Thomas Roberts	(25 years)	8 years penal servitude
William G. Stephenson	(21 years)	6 years penal servitude
James Ellison	(29 years)	6 years penal servitude
Oliver Sanderson	(25 years)	4 years penal servitude
William Muckle	(25 years)	4 years penal servitude
William Baker	(22 years)	4 years penal servitude

The men had short periods of incarceration in Durham, Leeds and Pentonville Prisons before finally being sent to Maidstone Prison to serve out their sentences.

The International Class War Prisoners' Aid organisation, and the N.U.M. paid for the defendants' barristers and provided cash to help support the prisoners' families during their sentences. They also paid the families' travelling costs to and from the prison. The last three prisoners were released after two years and three months, the others also after two-thirds of their sentences.

On release, Oliver Sanderson, William Muckle and William Baker went to a supporters' rally in Poplar and after a 'great weekend' in London travelled with their families to Newcastle by train. Crowds awaited them at the Central Station – and there were further celebrations at the 'Farmer's Rest public house. Money was 'hoyed into a hat' for them and then they made their way to Dudley where there was more partying, speeches and the presentation of commemorative medals which had on them an image of prison bars with an arm through waving a red flag. Finally, the released prisoners went in to the Co-operative Hall in Dudley where further presentations were made and sums of money handed to them.[157]

---

[157] Muckle, *Ibid*, pp.57–59. See also Hutcheson, Margaret, *Let no wheels turn – the wrecking of the Flying Scotsman, 1926*, (Washington, TUPS BOOKS, 2006).

CRAMLINGTON'S AIRSHIP

The Royal Naval Air Station, Cramlington (RNASC) started in 1918 and covered 155 acres which included 30 acres of camp buildings to the north of what became Nelson Village. The largest building was the 'Non-Rigid Hangar' – the airship shed, which was 100 yards in length. The air station was located at Cramlington to provide air patrols against German Zeppelins and submarines which harried North Eastern coastal towns and shipping. It was home to an airship squadron flying 'Coastal Class' non-rigid construction airships which were modelled on the French Astra-Torres design. They had a flying time of 22 hours and a top speed of 52 mph. Unfortunately, this type of airship suffered from different forms of instability and by the end of the First World War only two were serviceable.[158] In 1929 The Airship Development Company came into Cramlington to build a small airship which was to be used for advertising purposes. They took over the airship hangar built by the RNASC which had been built during the First World War but never used. It stood at the northern end of Nelson Avenue, Nelson Village.

The airship shed viewed from the south.

---

[158] Extracted from a draft report prepared by Alan Price-Talbot in May 2005 for Cramlington Yesterday Society.
[159] Image from Susan Napier's collection.

Construction work on the airship was carried out by specialists seamstresses from Cartington; these ladies worked on the gas envelope or bag. Beneath the airship a gondola was attached which had two seats, one for the pilot and one for the coxswain. When completed, the airship was inspected by an Air Ministry official and the first flight took place on 11th September 1929 under the control of Captain Weir. Walter Wilson's grocery chain was the first business to advertise using it. The airship was powered by a 60hp Hornet engine, which was later changed to a Rolls Royce Hawk engine with 75hp. The airship was 137 feet long with a 60,000 cubic feet envelope and a payload capacity of 700 lbs. The gondola was intended for two persons, but later it was fitted with a third cockpit. Unfortunately, the airship crashed while flying over Belgium in 1930. The pilot escaped unhurt but Airship AD1 GFAAX had to be scrapped.

The First World War Airship Station at Carpet Heath in June 1930.[160]

---

[160] Image from Susan Napier's collection.

CRAMLINGTON AERODROME

In 1915 The Royal Flying Corps (RFC) chose Cramlington for a small air station at the highest point of the village, at Beacon Hill three quarters of a mile from Plessey Checks.

The RFC equipped the station with BE2c (left) and Sopwith (right) spotter planes.

Later 36 (HD) Squadron was formed there prior to being posted to Seaton Carew. A succession of Reserve Squadrons – Nos. 46, 52 and 61 were formed there before they too were sent to their operational stations. In December 1917, 75 Training Squadron, which was later named 52 Training Depot Squadron RAF was formed at Cramlington.

Cramlington Aerodrome in the 1930s during the Kings Cup Air Race.[161]

RAF Cramlington closed in 1919. A year later it re-opened for commercial flying. Commercial and recreational flying was under the aegis of Cramlington Aero Club which was co-owned by two members – Connie Leathart and Leslie Runciman. Connie Leathard was one of England's pioneering women fliers who also flew with the wartime Air Transport Auxilliary. She was a friend of Amy Johnson who set many flying records in the 1930s. Cramlington Aero Club closed at the beginning of the Second World War.

---

[161] Image from Susan Napier's collection.

A Handley Page W8 giving a flying display at a 1932 Aero Club pageant at Cramlington.

George Clough at Cramlington Air Show. [162]

Mr. Leslie Miners, in a book published by Blyth Valley Council in 1996, provided details of his memories of Cramlington Airfield: *'The famous 'Kings Cup Air Race' included Cramlington Aerodrome. I saw Kingsford Smith, Jim Mollison and the famous pilot, who was later to become his wife – Amy Johnson. There were always long queues for a trip round the area which cost five shillings. The parachute drop was a very big attraction. In the 1930's it was a dangerous and precarious activity.'* [163]

---

[162] Reproduced with permission of Ian Clough.
[163] Griffin, Andy, *A Slice of Life – Fifty Years in the Blyth Valley – The People's Perspective*, (Blyth, Blyth Borough Council, 1996) p.136.

SPORT AND RECREATION

It is not difficult to imagine how important sport, especially that played on open fields in 'fresh' air, was to men who toiled, sometimes in 'bad air' hundreds of feet underground. For many men life was short and they knew that the dangers of mining could claim their life at any time so they made the most of what they had outside of home and away from work.

Gardening was important for creative and economic reasons, especially growing vegetables which helped to feed large families. Most of the mine workers' houses had long gardens. Being close to farms afforded ready access to quantities of manure and, through constant reworking of the soil, their gardens became productive of most species of vegetables.

Music too was important as an extension of chapel and church singing. Cramlington Male Voice Choir was particularly successful. Formed in 1934 it was the brain-child of Dick Seth and James Jackson who became the musical director. The choir had 50 members and won competitions at The Wansbeck Festival and at Stockton. It also featured in BBC radio broadcasts, the first being a programme called '*The History of Coal*' which was recorded at Cramlington Co-operative Hall. During the Second World War the choir performed to raise money for good causes such as The British Red Cross and Wings for Victory. A classic event involved the choir combining with several other local choristers to perform Handel's Messiah under the directorship of Harry Chenalle, the choir master of St. Nicholas Church. Many renowned artists 'guested' with Cramlington's Male Voice Choir, including Gladys Willis, Heddle Nash and Annitsford's own Owen Brannigan.

Cramlington Male Voice Choir in 1937. Jack Percival is third from the left in the back row. Jim Reed is third from the left at the front.[164]

---

[164] From Jack Raffle's collection.

Football played an important part in the lives of the men and they had some significant successes.

Shankhouse Blackwatch played their matches at Stickley Farm on a field provided by the tenant farmer Mr. Hogg. The team was named after the Black Watch Regiment which was billeted in Shankhouse before the First Boer War (1880–81) and some local men played for and against the military team.

Shankhouse Blackwatch 1884/85.

In the English F.A. Challenge Cup qualifying round in 1887 Shankhouse beat Scarborough 5 goals to 3 and then Darlington 2 goals to nil. They then had a bye to earn a plum home tie against the F.A. giants Aston Villa at St. James' Park. The Blackwatch team, playing in black and amber colours, put up a spirited show but were soundly beaten by the professionals by 9 goals to nil. The home team were Woods, Todd, Burlington, Riley, Todd, Ritson, Metcalf, Thompson, Matthews, Hamilton and Hedley.

In the F.A. Cup of 1893 Shankhouse were drawn away to Nottingham County where 5,000 spectators saw them go down 4 goals to nil. The team that day comprised Ord, Robson, Dowling, Rendle, Dick, Endean, Gibson, Matthews, Nicholson, Willis and McNally. Despite the failure in the F.A. cup, Shankhouse Blackwatch won the Northern Alliance title in 1893, to break the Sunderland A team's stranglehold of five successes in six seasons. They went on to clinch the Northumberland F.A. Senior Cup for the sixth time in 1895.

The goalkeeper Roger Ord, when aged 13, had played in the Northumberland Junior Cup Final and helped his team to win the trophy in successive years. He went on to play professionally for Middlesbrough; moved to Hebburn

Argyle and then transferred to Arsenal where he played for three years before transferring to Luton. He made 50 first team appearances in the Southern League between 1900 and 1902.

The above players were thought to be the most successful 'modern' team in the history of The Blackwatch, winning the Blyth and District league during the 1912-13 season. The team included – *Back row (left to right)*: **(G. Beattie), G. Telford, E. Isaacs, W. Endean, W. Patterson, (Unnamed), W. Waugh.** *Front row*: **J. Bartlett, A. Gray, G. Brown, (unnamed), A. Holland.**

Other members of the team were, J. Armstrong, R. Bickle, J. Bowman, G. Brown, P. Dodds, D. Evans, A. Grey, W. Hall, J. Hawke, J. Hoskin, J. Isaac, W. Isaac, R. Lumsden, J. Pellow, H. Neil, A. Stephens, A. Wheaton and W. Williams. Some of the players, like Roger Ord a decade earlier, went on to play professional football. These included: W. Isaac (Middlesbrough), E. Isaac (Leyton Orient), J. Isaac (Huddersfield), W. Isaac (Newcastle United), J.W. Stephens (Swindon Town), Alf Stephens (Leeds United), G. Brown (Aston Villa) and W. Waugh (Huddersfield).

The Shankhouse School team for 1927, proudly parading their strips.

Shankhouse School 1930–1931.

Back row (left to right): Burridge, Patterson, Langman. *Middle row*: Gordon, Mitchell, Mowat. *Front row*: Hardy, Forster, J. Isaac, J.W. Isaac, Hall.

Shankhouse School team 1932–1932.

Back row (left to right): Spry, Haggie, Johnson, Nesbit, Sowden, (Mr. Blackburn). *Middle row*: King, Parks, Mowat. *Front row*: Kelly, J. Stephens, W.J.Isaac, A. Stephens, Hyde.

In the 1930–31 season, the boys carried off the South Northumberland League Cup, the Cremona Shield, the Blake Cup and the Northumberland and Durham Schools Cup. Two hundred and sixty goals were scored and fifteen against, in 37 matches without defeat.

St. Nicholas Church team, c.1940.[165]

Back row (left to right): **Mr. Morrison (Manager Fox and Hounds), J. Davison, F. Stephen, A. Ferrow, Reg Ord, PC Andy Taylor, T. Hindmarsh, N. Brown, J. Hart.** *Middle row*: **George Appleby, T. Davison, Jack Morrison, B. Booth, J. Hindmarsh, B. Harm.** *Front row*: **Ted Waugh, J. Hume, J Cockburn, B. McIver, B. Caruthers.**

Cycling

Cramlington Bicyclists had a large following in the villages. Their minutes for 1879 show a formally established organisation with:

Captain	R. Bowman
Secretary	Thos. Bowman
Treasurer	G. Burlinson
Vice President	J. Parker
Committee	J. Cleminson, T. Smith, A. Fletcher, W. Weeks.

Mr. Potter, the Colliery Viewer was asked in September 1881 to allow colliery ground to be used as a track. The Bicyclists' minutes for October 25th 1881 list fourteen men who have signed or made their mark to an agreement to repay each of nine men the sum of £20 (when the funds were available) as reimbursement for the sum outlaid by them for laying the track. In 1883 the committee set about building a club dressing room with brick foundations 20 feet by 15 feet.

Successive minutes of the Bicyclists are interesting:

'Prizes not to exceed 10 shillings.'
'Each member to wear proper costume.'
'Any member using profane language during club outings, tours etc., shall be fined 3 pence for each offences. If he refuses to pay, he will be expelled from the club.'
'A night will be set apart to put the track right – cut the grass and thistles and spread the ash heaps.'
'Ten mile and other races will be under Wallsend track rules.'
'No member to be allowed to ride on a track after a frost gives way. Anyone breaking this rule will be fined 5 shillings.'

---

[165] Image supplied by Malcolm and Daphne Morrison.

Cricket

George Shum Storey of Arcot House was an enthusiastic cricketer and H.A. Taylor, the county archivist, presenting his historical survey of Cramlington in July 1963 wondered whether Shum Storey had been responsible for introducing the sport into the village at the beginning of the 19th century. If he had been it survived many decades as the image of the village's 1900's team shows.

Cramlington Cricket Club 1908.[166]

Galas and Treats

Ernest Fletcher Ord's autobiography takes us back to the beginning of the 20th century when he was a young boy. His father's pay day was Friday and if he was lucky he was given a penny to spend in Mrs. Ritson's shop at Shankhouse: *'Every Easter and Whit Monday, Mrs. Ritson used to wheel the sweets down from the shop to a field which belonged to farmer Ben Hogg, set up a stall and the children used to gather there and have ball games. … Here was born, maybe from Mrs. Ritson's idea that something should be done in a bigger way to give the children a day in their lives to remember, and that is how the children's gala day came about. It was suggested along with this, (the children's gala) that something should be done for the old people, and so began the old people's treat. The wives of the committee men worked and made a banner with which to head the procession … a band was hired from a neighbouring colliery. There were galloping horse roundabouts and the usual lot of coconut stalls and dolly shies along with a gift of money. It was a great success. All the children were given a cup of tea and a bag with cake. Sports of all kinds were held for all ages male and female, they carried on until dusk, and had to be continued the following Monday night. The old people's treat was mainly held in Spring time … in the hall above Shankhouse Co-op … and Mr. J.D. Forster, who had the shop n Station Terrace provided the vehicles for those who were unable to walk to the Hall. Local people would put on a concert and there would be tea.'*

Easter egg bowling. **Gala Day float.**

---

[166] This is thought to have been on Blagdon Estate.

Gala Day procession.

Old People's Treat on a sunny day.

CRAMLINGTON'S PROMINENT PEOPLE

In highlighting those people from Cramlington who have risen to greatness, let us remember that behind every successful man or woman there is often a legion of helpers who have guided the honoured person on their way. Often these people have been gifted in their own right and made massive contributions to community life without ever seeking for themselves honour or recognition. It is usually others who make judgements in measuring their achievements. In assembling this book I have been as guilty as anyone in deciding who and what should be included.

This final section includes just a few people who, in anybody's book on Cramlington, deserve a special mention.

ROBERT CLOUGH – inventor.

Robert Clough had a house and business at the Folly, West Cramlington. The family brewed beer, had a general dealers business and later a post office. They were probably best known for being manufacturing chemists. St. Nicholas Church Magazine for 1902 carried the advertisement below for Robert Clough's potions.

ROBERT CLOUGH
Manufacturer of

"Clough's Golden Pill of Health"

"Clough's Life Salts"

Baking Powder Etc.,

WEST CRAMLINGTON
The Trade Supplied

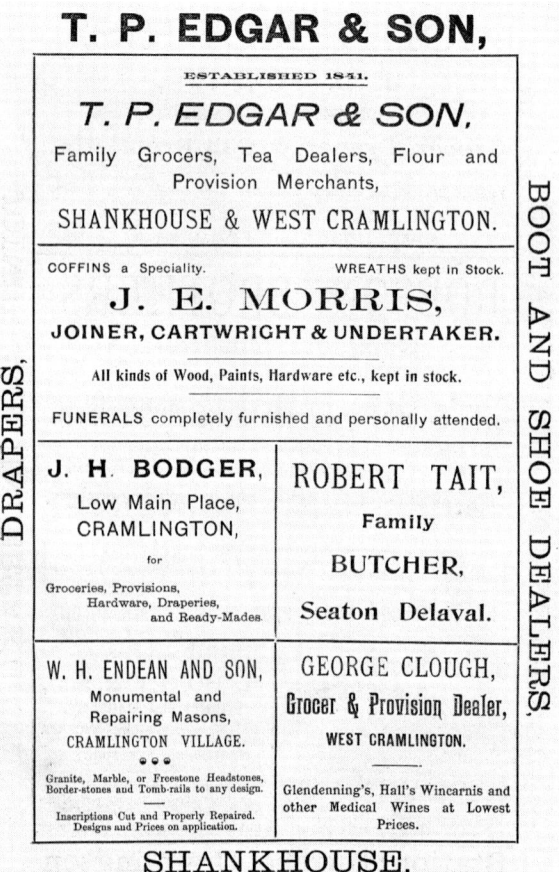

St. Nicholas Church's magazine for November 1912 carried an advert for George Clough's medicines.

George Clough was born on 23rd March 1856. Through his father's influence and guidance, he also manufactured herbal and chemical remedies.

In 2009, George Clough's grandson Ian wrote a small booklet entitled 'The Effervescent Cloughs of West Cramlington.' In this booklet, he drew together evidence and anecdote to substantiate the claim that his grandfather George Clough had been responsible for inventing Andrews Fruit (Liver) Salts.

One strand of evidence concerning Clough's invention was drawn from the written reminiscences of Ernest Fletcher Ord who had lived in Shankhouse Village: *'Another famous homemade doctor was George Clough who owned a property-cum-chemist shop at West Cramlington. He had a recipe which was to work wonders with a discontented stomach ... a small white powder in a paper twisted packet for one penny. This stomach cure eventually reached the ears of Scott and Turner, wholesale manufacturing chemist in Newcastle. They bought the recipe from George Clough and introduced it on the market.'* [167]

Scott and Turner's premises were opposite St. Andrew's Church in Newcastle, hence the name given to Clough's remedy.

The Clough family with the bearded George at the back.[168]

---

[167] Clough, Ian, *The Effervescent Cloughs of West Cramlington*, (Clough, 2010) p.11.
[168] Reproduced with permission of Ian Clough.

Mr. CHARLES FENWICK – M.P. for Wansbeck.

Charles Fenwick was born on 5th May 1850 at Paradise Row, in Cramlington. His father, John, was a miner. Charles attended the village school but received little formal education. He started his working life at 9 years of age, first on the surface then from age 10 he was underground working twelve to thirteen hours a day. When he was 17, he became a hewer and his shorter hours gave him the chance to study. In 1863 he joined the Northumberland Miners' Association and worked actively in his local association. In May 1876 he attended his first delegate meeting as a representative of Bebside at Blyth. In 1878 he was elected to the joint committee of the Northumberland Miners' Association and for a number of years was a member of its wages committee. He was made trustee of the association and was delegate at the Trade Union Congress at Aberdeen in 1844. The following year he was elected straight from the coal face to become the liberal MP for Wansbeck Division of Northumberland. He held this seat through eight successive general elections until his death. Throughout his Parliamentary career he continued to be closely associated with mining' activities and in 1887 he attended a four day conference in the Oddfellows Hall in Edinburgh which began on 11th October. There he represented 26,000 miners and was chosen as vice-president. The president was Thomas Burt.

Fenwick went to Paris to the International Trades Union Congress, which was meeting to discuss the question of shorter hours. As a Gladstonian Liberal, he was opposed to state intervention and maintained these attitudes to the end of his life.

He served on The Coal Dust Commission, the Secondary Education Committee for England and Wales, and in 1900 on the Inquiry into causes of injuries to railway servants. Later he became deputy chairman of the House of Commons and frequently presided over proceedings. In 1911 he was made Privy Councillor. On January 27th 1906, Charles Fenwick laid one of the foundation stones for the Aged Miners' Cottages situated opposite the railway station in Cramlington. He was married to Jane (née Gardener) from 1869 and together they had two sons. He died on 20th April 1918.

RICHARD FYNES –
miner, representative, author, entrepreneur – friend of humanity.

Richard Fynes was born on 7th April 1827 in Newcastle upon Tyne. His father and later his step-father were drunkards. Aged 8 Richard began work underground at St. Hilda's colliery at South Shields. Aged 10, to escape his bullying step-father he ran away to sea. Unfortunately, after eighteen months under the guidance of the captain of *The Ruby*, Richard fell overboard into the Thames. He contracted typhoid and after making a recovery returned to St. Hilda's Colliery.

Whilst at this pit a huge explosion killed 51 men and boys. Not long afterwards, in a pit in North Shields he wandered around lost underground for two days getting weak and hungry before eventually being found. These two events made a great impression on young Richard and from then he became active in the events which led to the great strike of 1844. Too young and too inexperienced to join the Union he became one of the trumpeters who led processions of miners to their meetings. In 1847 he went with a friend (Martin Jude) to the House of Commons with a petition by the miners to have inspectors appointed and to seek the prevention of the use of candles and gunpowder in 'fiery' pits. Although the petition was successful, the strike failed in its objectives and many miners, including Richard were refused their old jobs. He moved to pits at Percy Main, New Delaval then Seaton Delaval.

Following further abuse from his step-father, Fynes went back to sea; travelling principally to Russia and France with frequent stop-offs in London. Aged 22 he returned to the pits, working at Barrington, Sleekburn and Choppington. He didn't reach Cramlington until 1851 and it was there that he met Thomas Burt, who later became an M.P. Richard also joined the Temperance Society and became enchanted with Primitive Methodism. In 1853 he married Sarah Powell, a widow twelve years his senior, already with a daughter. He had no children of his own. Around this time he helped form the Miners' Provident Society (a Union by another name), becoming president. In 1862 he signed up for the Northern Reform Union. The Miners' Permanent Relief Fund started and Fynes urged every miner to enrol as it was intended to help miners and their widows after accidents or fatalities. He had properties in Cramlington and it was his buildings which were used to establish the Co-operative movement in Cramlington.

In 1861, through his influence over the workers, he helped quell industrial disputes at West Cramlington Colliery, but was later dismissed by the management because he was considered too influential. Out of work, he bought himself a horse and cart and commenced as a seller of fruit and vegetables, later developing this into a general dealer's business at Cowpen. Now as an independent businessman, he could recommence his efforts for miners. On Christmas Day 1862 he gathered together 3,000 to 4,000 men in a field at Horton. Here he called on them to resist the mine owners demands for two yearly binding system which was being reinstated after eighteen years absence. As a result of this meeting 'The Miners' Mutual Confident Association' was formed – as a precursor to the Miners' Union.

In 1865 Fynes branched out and bought the Octagon Chapel at Blyth and converted it into a music hall, theatre and place of entertainment. This proved highly successful and commercially profitable. With his friend Thomas Burt he campaigned against the MP for Morpeth, Sir George Gray; Burt his younger protégé subsequently being elected.

In 1873 Richard Fynes influential book *The Miners of Northumberland and Durham – a history of their social and political progress'*, was published. In his preface he wrote: *'Many writers have endeavoured – some of them in a supercilious and patronising fashion – to give the public a notion of the peculiar traits and habits of miners, and whilst many of them have been successful in this respect, none of them have yet, to my knowledge, attempted to give any account of their doings, their sufferings, and their struggles, in the assertion of their social and political independence.*

With a view to supplying this deficiency, I have set myself to work, feeling to some measure qualified for the task in consequence of having spent all, except the last few years of my life in the pits. I have passed through all the grades of mining from being a trapper boy behind a door to a hewer at the face and have therefore had many opportunities of witnessing the dangers, hardships and drudgery of a miner's life; whilst I have also seen or heard, or read of the glorious deeds done by men who are well nigh forgotten.' [169]

Despite being removed from pit-work, Fynes continued to push for the two shaft system in collieries.

Meanwhile his theatre became one of the largest in the north, sufficient to accommodate 2,500 patrons. In 1882, at the Mechanics Institute, Blyth (now the library) he entertained 30 veterans of the miners' early battles for justice. In September 1892, following his death, a special train had to be commissioned to take the thousands of people who knew him to attend his funeral in Blyth. It was said of Richard Fynes, that *'Those who had known him the longest, loved and admired him the most.'* At his graveside, Thomas Burt M.P., said of Fynes, that his friend *'had been a friend of humanity.'*

---

[169] It is difficult to imagine how someone who left school at 12 could educate himself so well that he could write with such scholarship, authority, clarity and wisdom.

MARY ANN SMITH – Canadian Politician.

Mary Ellen Smith (née Spear) was born in Cornwall on 11th October 1861. She arrived in Cramlington as a child when her father came with the strike breakers in 1865. She showed great promise as a student and as a young elementary school teacher married a widower, Mr. Ralph Smith of Holywell. In 1891, Ralph became ill and during his convalescence he and his wife emigrated to Vancouver.

Ralph took an active part in politics becoming an M.P. in British Columbia and then in the Canadian Parliament. As his career progressed, Mary Ellen was constantly beside him on speaking platforms. She campaigned on behalf of women and children and was responsible for the building of hospitals and promoting the suffrage movement. In 1916 Ralph Smith returned to the British Columbia Parliament but in 1917 he died very suddenly.

By popular acclaim, Mary Ellen succeeded him as an M.P. She introduced a female minimum wage act and regulations concerning maternity leave and introduced a bill to provide pensions for mothers with dependent children whether divorced, widowed or single. She contended that there were no illegitimate children. *'There may be illegitimate parents, but in God's name do not let us brand the child.'*

In 1920 she became a cabinet minister without portfolio, the first woman to reach this position within a British Empire Parliament. In 1923, the Department of Immigration sent her to England to lecture on the benefits of her new country – *'Canada is a desirable country for future settlement.'* She carried a placard which read – 'Canada Needs You.' Mary Ellen Smith died on 3rd May 1933 in Vancouver, British Columbia.

HARRY HUTCHINS – Ann Pit, Cramlington.

Harry Hutchins was born at Harrow-barrow, Cornwall in 1864. He was the son of a miner and came with his parents to Cramlington in 1873. He attended the Seaton Delaval Presbyterian School until he was 12 and then commenced work underground at Ann Pit as a trapper lad. At the age of 15 he suffered a serious injury to his left foot which had to be amputated. Unable to work, he returned to school at East Cramlington until he was 18. He then returned to the colliery and despite his disability did several jobs underground. In 1919 the men appointed him check-weighman and later Secretary. For many years he acted as local compensation secretary and was widely considered to be the best informed person on compensation in the county.

Harry Hutchins was secretary to the Joint Accident Fund for Cramlington Collieries; chairman of the Group Committee and secretary and chairman of the Funeral Hearse Fund. He was deputy landlord for the Northumberland Association for Miners Homes for the Aged in Cramlington and also served on the Urban Council. He was an active Labour Party member and a staunch Primitive Methodist, being a Church trustee and Sunday School teacher, On his death, the *Morpeth Herald* reported that more than one thousand people attended his funeral.[170]

OWEN BRANNIGAN – opera singer.

Owen Brannigan was born on 10th March 1908 in Annitsford. His father, who was of Irish descent, was organist at St. John the Baptist Roman Catholic Church, Annitsford from 17 years of age. Young Owen began his singing career at the church as a boy soprano. In 1929 Owen Brannigan moved south to look for work and he began singing as an amateur while continuing his career as a joiner in Slough. In his spare moments he appeared with the Windsor Operatic Society. In 1934 he enrolled as a night student at the Guildhall School of Music while working as a

---

[170] Extracted from Davison, John, *Northumberland Miners History 1919–1939*, (Cambridge, Buckle, 1973) p.142

government clerk. Four years later he was a bass singer at Westminster Cathedral. He was singled out in a cathedral performance by Sir Landon Ronald and was offered a scholarship to continue his studies. In 1942 he won the Guildhall's Gold Medal. During the Second World War he was in charge of construction work, building army camps, but was still able to make some broadcasts for the BBC. As a result he was invited to join Sadler's Wells Opera, with whom he made his professional operatic debut at the age of 35 as Sarastro in Mozart's *The Magic Flute*. He was with Sadler's Wells between 1944 and 1949 and again from 1952 to 1958. He performed at the Glyndebourne Festival Opera from 1947 and at Covent Garden in 1947, 1948 and 1958. He appeared in the 1953 film *The Story of Gilbert and Sullivan* and in several Gilbert and Sullivan concerts at the Proms. He was probably better known as an oratorio than as an opera singer and his repertoire ranged from Purcell to Bach's *B Major Mass*. He sang solos in Haydn's *Creation*, Handel's *Messiah* and Verdi's *Requiem*. Owen Brannigan recorded all of his major roles under the composer's baton; for Sir Malcolm Sargent he recorded many of his Gilbert and Sullivan roles; and for the D'Oyly Carte Opera Company, in 1968 he recorded the Pirates of Penzance.

He was awarded the O.B.E. in 1964. In 1972 he was involved in a road traffic accident from which he never fully recovered and died on 9th May 1973 from pneumonia, aged 65. He is buried in St. John the Baptish Roman Catholic churchyard at Annitsford.

ALFRED WILLIAM SMITH – Scout, Churchman, historian.

Alf Smith was born on 3rd November, 1898 at Broomhill in Northumberland. His elementary education was at Westmoor, Forest Hall ending aged 14 when he left to start work as a blacksmith for the Co-op in Cramlington. His further education began almost immediately when his former head teacher, Mr. Davison, who was running night classes, sent him to Professor McDonald at Newcastle for tuition in literature. After completing his apprenticeship he was recommended for the post of education welfare officer in Cramlington and Delaval District, a role he held until 1963.

As a youngster Alf attended Lord Baden-Powell's second scout camp and thereafter he remained faithful to the Scouting movement. After military service in the First World War he became an instructor, examiner, district and group scout master. In 1933 he was appointed assistant district commissioner for Dinnington and Seaton Burn and later became district commissioner for Seaton Valley. By 1955 he was assistant county commissioner and at this time his long service was recognised through the presentation of the Silver Acorn and Silver Wolf awards. He retired from active Scouting in 1966 but continued to hold the position of honorary scout commissioner and district president for Seaton Valley.

During the whole period of his commitment to Scouting, Alf Smith was equally committed to his local community in Cramlington. He was an active member of St. Nicholas Church as bell-ringer, Sunday School and youth leader, and for much of the time was church warden and parochial church council member. He later held the position of church warden emeritus. During the Second World War he was a Commando and later performed secret duties guarding the King and Queen at Balmoral. In peacetime, for about ten years, he was secretary and treasurer for Seaton Valley Association for the Blind; and a member, then chairman, of the Cramlington Old People's Treat Committee, a position he held for 20 years.

Alf Smith was an authority on Cramlington and much requested as a public speaker. For the centenary of St. Nicholas Church in 1968 he wrote '*The Story of Cramlington*', a booklet giving an historical overview of the town's development since Roman times. He was also a gifted oil painter and a skilled craftsmen working with wood and iron. In 1927 Alf married Ida Taylor at Bedlington and together they had two children, Brenda and Valerie. Alf's beloved wife Ida died in 1977. He died on 20th August 1990 aged 91. Alfred William Smith was a man who never consciously sought publicity or recognition for himself, but those people who shared parts of his life considered themselves richer for the experience.

ALAN LOWTHER – teacher, artist, poet, local historian.

Alan Lowther was born in Cramlington on 5th August, 1927. He attended the local grammar school before going to Kings College, Newcastle where he graduated with honours in German. After several years as a year-group teacher, he became headmaster at the Cathedral School in Newcastle, a post he held for seventeen years.

Alan's father had been a Methodist lay preacher, but with his father's blessing Alan broke with tradition and was confirmed into the Church of England at Horton Church, situated marginally outside the parish of Cramlington. For many years he was a communicant member of St. Nicholas Church where he assisted at the Eucharist and held the position of church warden.

Alan remained single. He was a linguist, artist, photographer, poet, calligrapher, musician, historian and founder member of Cramlington Yesterday and Cramlington Local History Society. His published books of poems include: *Stations of the Cross, Bible Journey, Floral Landscapes, Cramlingtuna and Blyth Valley – a Millennium Celebration.*

He died on 4th February 2008 and is buried in the Village Cemetery. A tribute paid at his funeral recorded that: *'Alan will be remembered for his contribution to community life; and the record he kept along with his books of poetry will provide a permanent reminder of his love of scripture and of literature.'*

DEVELOPMENT OF THE NEW TOWN

The story of Cramlington's development from 1950 onwards would need a book twice as long as this one, but it would be wrong to finish without acknowledging some of the key changes which have occurred.

In 1951 almost 75% of local employment in south east Northumberland was in coal mining but this was predicted to drastically decline, which of course it did. In 1958 the County Planning Committee considered that Cramlington, located favourably beside rail, road, air and shipping transport links, was the most suitable place for residential development as a New Town, with the proposed creation of additional acommodation for at least 10,000 people. In 1962 it was agreed that 170 acres known as Bassington Farm should be aquired for industrial development. On 8th January 1963 the master plan for the New Town was approved by the Minister of Housing and Local Government and two months later the foundation stone of Wilkinson Sword's factory was laid by the Rt. Hon. Frederick J. Errol, the then president of the Board of Trade. A further 350 acres of land was aquired adjacent to Nelson Village which drew in a further ten industrial units.

Cramlington was proclaimed a New Town in 1964; the aim being to build 16,000 houses, fifteen primary and twelve senior schools, sixteen public houses and 500 acres of industrial sites. The industrial development in the north west of the town, and the construction of roads and infrastructure linked to the south by a spine road leading to the Tyne Tunnel, were to be under the auspices of Northumberland County Council.

With 600 employees, Wilkinson Sword was the first factory to open. 25 years later there were 93 seperately occupied industrial units across sites at Bassington, Nelson, South Nelson, East Hartford and Windmill. Industrial estates, with thirteen further units in East Cramlington, Nelson Village and South Cramlington employing in total 5,500 people.

House building began in 1965 with the construction of 152 flat-roofed properties by Hawthorn Leslie in the Hall Close estate, close to the old village centre.

Cramlington Development Corporation came into being in the early 1960s with builders J.T. Bell (later Bellway) and William Leech (later Beazer group) having the remit to build private dwellings – flats, terraced, semi-detached and detached homes in the Collingwood, Whitelea and Southfield areas of the town and later in Mayfield, Parkside, Shankhouse, Beacon Hill and Barns Park.

Parkside, 1984.

In November 1972 a new library was opened and alongside it a new health centre was built. In 1977 the Queen officially opened the Concordia Sports Centre. A new shopping centre was built in Dudley Lane on the site of the former market garden with its red bricked dwelling which is now Lal Qila, Indian restaurant.

The prediction in 1970 was that Cramlington would eventually have a population of 62,000. In 2013 the town had a population in excess of 39,000.